Evolve Your
COACHING
BUSINESS

The Ultimate Guide to Success
Doing the Work You Love

KAT KNECHT

CEO Soul Driven Success, CPCC, PCC

ISBN: 978-19-5-315345-6

Published by

If you are interested in publishing through Lifestyle Entrepreneurs Press,
write to: Publishing@LifestyleEntrepreneursPress.com

Publications or foreign rights acquisition of our catalog books.
Learn More: www.LifestyleEntrepreneursPress.com

Printed in the USA

CONTENTS

INTRODUCTION

As a coach who is passionate about the positive impact you can have on this world, I congratulate you for choosing this book. It shows a willingness to do some work, both inner and outer, to evolve your business and yourself.

It takes courage to be a coach; to engage with other humans in the areas closest to their hearts. It is a funny business to be in, for sure. Not only are you connecting with people in such an intimate and personal way, but you are also asking them for money!

This is one of the aspects of the coaching profession that I haven't always liked. I once thought I would rather have someone else be in control of bringing me clients or contracts, so I could focus on the coaching work I loved so much. How about you? Has that ever crossed your mind?

What I have discovered, and what inspired me to put pen to paper, is that growing and evolving a coaching business is the best personal growth work I know of. It brings coaches to the edge of their greatness. Over and over, coaches are asked to face their fears, accept failure as a part of the deal, and celebrate the big and small successes along the way.

You are reading this book because you care about this world. You are up for doing some of the hard things needed to accomplish something lasting and worthwhile.

I have put my heart and soul into the pages of this book for the same reason. I care about this world, and I believe the coaching profession can bring to it a much-needed transformation; one client, one coaching group, one program delivered to a few or many at a time.

I hope you will not only read this book, but that something within the book (perhaps one of the many exercises or maybe a story or two that resonate with you) will spur you to inspired action and help you evolve your coaching business, a little or a lot. Because it matters to me, and to others, that you do.

The inspiration for this book began over twenty years ago when I decided to become a coach. It was a book, *The 7 Habits of Highly Effective People*, and a coaching program associated with it, that gave me my entry into the coaching world.

I experienced how powerful it is to have a book I could hold in my hands and a coach to guide me as I learned and practiced the wisdom found within the pages. The next step on my journey to becoming a coach was the co-active coaching book I read cover to cover before beginning my coach training.

As a matter of fact, my first coach training supervisor had written a book about the coaching business. It had some helpful information, but it didn't resonate with me on a heart level.

The facts were good enough but, if I was going to take the leap from working on an executive team at the US Postal Service to a career as a coach and entrepreneur, I wanted something more than facts to guide me.

There have been other books written about the business side of coaching that I have enjoyed and benefited from, but there was always something missing for me.

SOUL

A lot has changed in the twenty years since I first experienced the *7 Habits* coaching program. Coaching has grown as a profession and now includes hundreds of thousands of coaches all over the world. What has not changed is the internal (and external) struggle between the burning desire to have a thriving coaching practice and the dread of taking the action needed to actually get clients!

I kept hearing about the same issues from the students I taught in the Co-Active Training Institute's certification program. I heard similar stories from my coaching colleagues. Things like, "I don't want to have to market my coaching...it's hard to get clients. The business side of coaching sucks."

I understood because I had my own struggles creating a sustainable coaching business over these twenty years. I failed at more than one iteration of my business. I am writing this book because I also succeeded in the evolution of my business, and it has brought me financial success that resonates with my soul.

By you reading this book, there is no guarantee you will become rich, though you very well may. You are not likely to completely bypass the challenges, though you might find them easier than ever before.

There is no promise that you will be an overnight success. But when you DO succeed, I am promising you will be happy.

The purpose of this book is to help you create the kind of success that supports your true calling.

To that end, I bring to these pages the lessons from my days in the trenches. It holds insights from the many training programs and super-duper mentors who have taught me buckets over the years, and stories of clients I have had the honor to work with.

As my nature compels me to do, I have tracked what works and what doesn't in all areas of my life. I am intentional about everything I do, to the point that it drives some people nuts! Just ask my husband!

My experience with my coaching business has been one of the great love affairs of my life. I have used this quirk of mine fully, and with passion.

This is what gives me faith that this book will be a benefit to you.

At the end of each section, you will find what I call "nuggets." These bits of wisdom and information have been gleaned from my many years of coaching. I hope you will find them useful and inspiring.

I also offer support beyond what you will read in the book. There are interactive exercises you can do online, and you will have access to live help when you need it.

There is a community of coaches (some who have already done the work and built successful coaching businesses, and some who are just beginning the journey) to support you as you evolve your business from wherever it may be now.

I have done my best to pare down all that I could have included in this book. I integrated the business building stuff with the soul work a coach needs in order to stay true to themselves. All this has been done so that you can be nourished on that deep level required to be there for your own clients and community.

My intention is for you to use this book as a guide. To trust it to take you where you want and need to go as a coach in your own business evolution, with the knowledge that others have paved the way and are here to cheer you on as you step into your own version of soul-driven success.

Part 1:

HEART AND SOUL

The greatest danger for most of us is not that our aim is too high and we miss it. Rather, it's that we aim too low and we reach it.
—Michelangelo

The job is not the work, what you do with your heart and soul is the work.
—Seth Godin

As a coach, where else is there to start than with the heart and soul? It is as true for building your business as it is when working your special brand of coaching magic with your clients. In this section, we delve into the power of vision—discovering your vision, inhabiting it and evolving it with a working plan that starts with what you have. Along the way, I will share some of my stories and experiences with visioning. And before you leave this section, you will have your own "successful business story," a story based on your business values which will help guide you to believe in your vision with all your heart and soul.

The Power of Vision

My husband, Curtis, and I were walking up the hill at the Ventura Botanical Gardens. It was one of those amazing winter days in central California. The rains had come and everything looked and smelled clean. The sun was shining and reflecting light on the ocean below us.

This hill is one of our sacred places. The place where we go when we are creating something new. We had walked this hill hundreds of times before, brainstorming ideas, imagining how we wanted an aspect of our life and our business to be if we could have it any way we wanted and clearing mental blocks that are a natural part of success of any kind.

On this day, much of the walking and talking centered on our coaching business, since that is one of our most precious creations. We were in high spirits and began imagining a vision we'd held for a long time.

Our conversations went something like this:

Imagine that we are guiding a community of coaches who are as committed as we are to bringing a positive change to the world. Yes! And imagine our tribe coming together every week on group calls and having our own transformative program that includes practical business training and the soul work we love so much.

How exciting! Even better, imagine we have a well-oiled machine behind the scenes, running the marketing so we have new people signing up for our program on a regular basis.

And a book that brings my love of teaching and storytelling together with my love of writing! Imagine that I am a sought-after coach for organizations I admire.

Imagine our income being so solid we rarely think about it, except to make sure we are managing it well.

By the time we reached the summit of our walk, we were both laughing at these imaginings which at one point in our lives would have seemed far-fetched. What had us laughing most was the fact that all of this was actually happening to us right then. What we were "imagining" was OUR REAL LIFE — the amazing manifestation of visioning we had done many years before and adjusted all the years in between.

I have found that in creating a successful business it is essential to have a vision that comes from your heart. And to listen to your soul as you set intentions along the way to keep you moving, step by step toward that bigger dream.

I know many of you want to jump right into the nuts and bolts of building a business, but this wouldn't be a heart-centered coaching book if we didn't first talk about intentions and visions.

I've seen so many businesses fizzle out because not enough time (or any time) was spent on imagination. What do YOU really want? What can't you live without? What gets you excited? What is your Bigger Vision for your business and for your life?

Now is the time for you to create your vision. In this chapter I will give you lots of tools to help you get there!

It Takes Both Art and Science

There is an art and science to everything.

In this case, the "science" includes the proven business strategies that work specifically for a coaching business, which I cover in the Marketing Your Way and Business Essentials part of the book. As much as you might be tempted, skipping over the science or racing to it or through it are not advised!

As important as the science is, the "art" comes first. Here, the art is HOW you want to create your business or the vision you have for creating your business. A vision holds the essence of how you want to evolve your business. It is the foundational structure that will ensure your coaching business comes from the heart and is guided by the soul.

I have used this visioning process and honed it for twenty years in order to get it to the place it is now as one of my central creation tools. It is the number one activity that has ensured my business success.

I have not only used it for myself, but with hundreds of others. In my work as a business and relationship coach, there were many people who found true love, others found business and life success. I guess you could say I have helped people visualize and realize their work, houses, and spouses!

Creating a successful business from a vision is exactly the same as any other kind of visioning. Like all areas of life, there are some things that seem very doable and others that seem impossible.

This is where the power of visualization works like no other process I know. The kind of vision I am going to unpack in this chapter with stories, examples, and exercises (to help you make your vision a reality) includes special qualities that I often see missing when people think of making a dream come true.

The Navigation Creation System

Before I break down the visioning process, I want to tell you the backstory of the imagining I was enjoying on that hill on a bright February day, and how I was guided by my vision.

A number of years before, while walking down the bike path where we live in Ojai, Curtis and I were talking about our business.

I had been successful for many years on my own while Curtis worked full time. We eventually transitioned into becoming business partners.

We started talking about our vision, imagining what we wanted our business to look like, and what we would be doing that would thrill us. The income and the output.

There were several things that rose to the top on that walk. We wanted a community of our own. We wanted to collaborate with kindred spirits. We wanted a good income, as well as a good personal life with lots of time for ourselves, our friends, and our families.

We had just published a book, so we imagined having a book at the center of our business. This was a big dream, for me in particular, since I love to write. Curtis imagined being in charge of the systems and structures that make the business tick. This had been his long-held dream.

That winter, we sat by the fire and visioned for hours. To make our vision a reality, we used a process I came up with years before called "The Navigation Creation System."

We started with what we had and with what we already knew worked for us — our strengths, passions, and credibility in the marketplace. Using the visioning tools and techniques I love most, we made a vision board that held the most important elements. We wrote a vision story that had us imagining this vision, not only at the end point, but how the journey might be as well.

At the center of our vision board was a church. Having recently been ordained as an interfaith minister, I imagined we would have a spiritual community of some sort.

Once we had the basic elements in place, we went looking for help. No vision worth achieving can be successful without partnership!

With a wonderful business consultant guiding us, we began building a platform for this new business venture.

As we began to take action, we checked in with our vision for inspiration and to see if we were aligned. Our vision helped us stay true to the essence of what we wanted.

During this time, we were super excited, and we were taking a lot of action toward making this vision a reality. Yet, nothing seemed to be working the way we had hoped.

Nothing, nada, not a single thing seemed to be happening in the real world. This was discouraging, to say the least.

As we looked at the vision we had created with such passion, I soon realized that something was missing. But I just didn't know what.

I knew I needed to have hands-on help with running my business. My vision was calling me forth into new territory. The land of the unknown.

Out of the blue, I received a call from a lovely woman reminding me that I had expressed interest in a business retreat being held in Los Angeles in a couple of weeks. She asked if I was planning to attend and talked to me about what I would learn.

Something sparked in me as she spoke. My soul said, "YES! This will help you with your vision." At the retreat, I signed up for a year-long program to help me see what was missing in my vision and business plan, and to keep me moving forward in my work.

I learned years ago that when a vision isn't becoming real there are two things to consider.

One is that visions never, ever come to fruition on our timeline! Some things I have envisioned have taken decades to happen, while others have miraculously materialized instantaneously.

Two is to look where you have become attached to the form and not the essence. Our minds like to make up the form we think will be best for us. Our soul is always guiding us to expand and grow, which means traveling into the unknown, being uncomfortable and being vulnerable. These are NOT things we usually run toward with glee.

This is the paradox. Reconciling a vision that holds your dream and the reality that your REAL dream is probably not going to look or happen as you think it will. Visioning requires holding the tension of this paradox.

During the year-long business program, I had an epiphany. The type that occurs when I let go of what I think is right and open to my inner guidance.

I still remember that moment with crystal clarity. My beautiful vision board with the church in the middle was in my view. I also saw the elements that were important—community, kindred spirits, a well-oiled machine, income, and open time.

I was exploring options on my niche, which I had done many times, and I thought I was pretty well dialed in.

But when I really opened up and used both sides of my brain— the practical side that knew my strengths and talents and the creative side that knew my passions—a new niche flashed before my eyes and changed everything.

My vision got a makeover. I found a new picture depicting a business academy and pasted it over the church.

Now the vision was different, and I could feel the missing piece had been discovered. It was not at all what I thought it would be!

My niche became even more specific as I stayed in action around my vision, and things started to happen.

I began attracting my ideal people.

This is how the visioning process works. It is not one and done or a dream you put on a board or hold in your heart as set in stone. A vision will guide you if you engage and pay attention. It is alive and will change and grow as you move forward taking the steps to make it a reality.

At its best, a vision holds the energy of what is in your heart and soul. The pictures, the colors, and the story all hold the essence of what will make you happy. True happiness that includes your soul's wisdom. Success that honors your values.

My vision was coming into reality. Another year passed and I created a new vision board that was simpler than ever before. This one held only the essence of my vision.

I had learned to let go of some of the superficial things and to focus less on how I thought it should look.

I paid attention to the signals from my soul and what was working to grow this stage of my business. I tracked the things that were happening. That part was fun!

Yet again, I worked on that ongoing lesson of PATIENCE. Despite things in my vision not happening as fast as I had expected they would, I knew it was the right vision because of the way I felt when I imagined my vision as reality. I kept moving forward with my marketing and the building of my program.

It was exciting and frustrating in equal measure as I homed in, iterated, and experimented with structure. I had success. I had failure. I had many learnings. I felt my vision moving forward, slowly but surely, as my business grew.

Now I knew the biggest work to be done was the inner work. In my vision story, I handled it all with ease and confidence. In the real world, it was a lot messier.

With the beginning of success came fear. "This seems like a lot of work! Would I be able to keep it going? What if I crashed and burned?"

I was called to a higher level of spiritual growth. To spend more time in meditation than ever before. To retreat to nature.

I hired a therapist to help me with the blocks. She met me where I was and encouraged me to shine my light as bright as possible. To feel all the fears and doubts...AND step into my greatness. That was huge!

My vision becoming a reality would require a whole new level of leadership. It called on me to find the help I needed while guiding my business partner and the team I was now assembling to make this well-oiled machine run.

By the time Curtis and I hit the Botanical Garden trail on that February day and playfully "imagined" our vision that had become real life, it had been three years since I first glimpsed this vision of my business.

That vision had evolved and changed in form, and yet, at its essence, remained the same.

I now had the community I dreamed of. A community of coaches, it turned out, who were passionate about their work in the world. I also had the marketing systems, the income, and the spaciousness that are a requirement for my joy. The big surprise to me was the book at the center. It was not my first book that I mentioned earlier, but the book you now hold in your hands.

Make It Real

A lesson about visioning landed in my lap with a great big thud, at the end of my startup phase of coaching many years ago.

I was yearning to have sustainable success.

I created a beautiful vision for my coaching business that year. I loved what I imagined could happen as I wrote my vision story and created an inspiring collage.

I thought about the following year and how happy I would be with a full roster of clients, full enrollment in my group programs, and perhaps a little book to sweeten the pot.

I put that dream out into the future and then got busy with the stuff of life.

As I do every year, that November I sat down to review the year that had just passed. I brought out my vision board and was sad to see that little I had visioned had been made real.

Here is the lesson: I had forgotten one of the cardinal rules of visioning.

Some of your vision's aspects are future oriented, of course, but much of what is included in a vision are things you need to start living right now.

I had not stayed engaged with my vision. In fact, I had ignored it and instead stayed in my comfort zone.

Along the lines of manifesting is the concept called "Acting As If." You need to inhabit your vision. Immerse yourself in it. Not in the future. But RIGHT NOW.

To make visioning more fun and effective, here are some ways to "be the change you want to see" in your successful business vision.

To inhabit the emerging truth of yourself and invite those sleeping aspects of who you REALLY are to "wake up and smell the coffee!" Here are six ways to do just that.

1. Act the Part

Act out your absolute best self; the one in your vision, the one who has already realized the dream. Have you heard the coaching question, "Who do you need to be?" Think about that and start being that person right now.

Go deep into the experience in as many ways as you can, as if it has already happened.

Acting As If is not magically creating something that doesn't exist or pretending that something absent is present.

It is waking up and inhabiting those aspects of yourself that are already present inside you. I mean your soul, your highest and best self, your destiny, and your truth. Your natural abilities and expertise you have acquired.

You could not conceive of them if they didn't exist somewhere inside you. You couldn't know them in others if they weren't a part of you.

Act as if your vision is already a done deal.

Here is an example. I had a vision of leading coaching circles. I wasn't sure what action to take so the first thing I did was to name my coaching circle and block out times and dates in my calendar for three months—AS IF the coaching circle was a done deal.

Then, during those time blocks, I would work on the coaching group. Sometimes I would work on the content or structure. Other times I would just sit and imagine exactly how I wanted that group to be. I was taking little steps forward.

After a few weeks, the coaching group was feeling more and more real. I started talking to people about it AS IF it *were* real. I was going to do this thing!

Then, the magic happened. I received a request to start a coaching group. The woman wanted it for herself, and she knew a few women she thought would be interested.

I was off to the races! I chose one of the dates on my calendar that I had already penciled in and invited her and her friends to my coaching group. I reached out to a few women I knew as well.

I had already done the work of choosing a name, I had a sound enough structure and content, and now with actual people interested, I was inspired to make this real. This coaching circle lasted more than a decade!

2. Visualize

Imagine yourself enjoying your ideal business success.

Imagine your clients and program participants. Picture people you enjoy and who resonate with you. Visualize the people you work with engaging with you just as you would like them to. Imagine yourself as the coach or leader you want to be.

You can do this by using a journal to simply daydream on paper.

Make sure your visualizations are based on your values. Include images of you acting as your authentic self, not some version you think you should be.

Pay attention to how you feel when you imagine your vision of reality. Be sure to visualize the small, sweet details.

When you hit a place that brings up fear, take a look before you move it out.

You are looking for that feeling of, "YES!!! This is me at my happiest, highest, most fulfilled, and satisfied state of being in my work. The people, the income, the impact." Even if it feels scary.

The tricky part is that only you can know what feels "just right" for you. Trust your heart. Go for that vision.

3. Add Structure

Gather some items that represent your vision and with which you resonate.

Spend time making a collage or another visual creation to help you stay "in the picture" of the vision. Our minds love images, metaphors, colors, sounds, and textures. Place your creation where you will see and engage with it often.

I often have my vision structures in the space where I do my planning. Where I get ready to take action or seek guidance on what to do next.

When you tune into the art of your vision, it will help with the science and foster the "what to do" that comes from that higher plane of existence.

Write your story using present tense—or even better, past tense since it's already a done deal!

(I have included an exercise at the end of this chapter, titled My Successful Business Story. I demonstrate how using your values to create an image and story will make your vision not only seem more real, it will actually help your vision *become* more real).

When you imagine living out your vision, what are you wearing? What does your hair look like? Your wardrobe? How do you feel in your own skin? What do you see in the mirror? How does your body move? What kind of self-care do you imagine?

These are all things you can control. Right now. These are all important aspects to honor as you inhabit this vision.

Here is an example of how this played out for me. I was ready to *really* take my business out into the world. I wanted to speak at the front of a room, to talk about things I cared deeply about. Before I booked those gigs or set foot in that room, I went on a shopping trip. You might think I was just looking for an excuse to buy new clothes. You might be right!

But what I found was that when I imagined the impact I wanted to have, I also imagined the way I looked and how good I felt in my own skin. Wearing the outfit of my future self you might say. This made the confidence real, present day. With that confidence, booking my first speaking gigs was easy. The people I reached out to said yes. I believe it was in part because how I felt about myself came through in our conversations. I had dressed the part and now I had the part!

4. Choose New Habits

This is a Biggy. In order to make a vision real, it requires new ways of being and doing. The easiest way to take action, the kind that makes a vision real, is to transform those actions into habits. Teeny-tiny, consistent action steps.

Choose activities that include the being and doing side of making your vision real. If you make it a habit, you will be guaranteed to succeed at creating a visionary life. Not just the one you have dreamed of while reading this chapter, but all the ones that come after.

Now is the time to create new habits to help you stay focused on your vision and take the action steps needed to make it real.

5. Surround Yourself with Cheerleaders

The people in our lives have a huge impact on how we feel and behave.

If there are people in your life who are more likely to support your limiting beliefs than your empowered ones, this is a good time to let them go.

On the flip side of this, it is also a great opportunity to seek out those who are a match for your best self.

Connect with new friends, old friends, family, and other kindred spirits. Engage with a community that will support this new vision.

Not everyone will understand what you are doing. A coaching business can sound like a risky proposition to some people. The people in your life may want you to play it safe. Though this is understandable, spend your time with those who are able and willing to cheer you on.

6. Share Your Vision with Others

It is essential that you share your vision of creating a successful coaching business with the cheerleaders in your life.

Inhabiting your vision in the ways described here will enable you to begin communicating to others what is in your heart in a way that is inviting to them. This is because it will come from a confident and grounded place in you.

Ground yourself in your new habits of embodying your vision. Know the truth it reveals about you, and the life you are choosing to live now and into the distant future.

A Working Plan

I recommend you create a "Working Plan" for your vision. One that you continually iterate. Checking in with your vision will remind you of the bigger picture and that always makes it easier to know what steps to take. It will also give you inspiration when you feel like procrastinating or giving up.

A working plan is simply that—it is roadmap that can be ever-changing and expanding, but also has elements that always stay the same. I believe you see a vision that seems wonderful and right as it comes to you. AND, at any given time, you will not have all the information about how it will look, the timing, the effort needed, and the unknown factors.

Write down some of the aspects of the what, how and when of making your vision a reality. Then as you move forward, check in often with this working plan. Allow yourself to get messy, scribble things out and put new things in as you gain information along the way. Make adjustments, and plan the steps to take next. It could be a weekly habit where you spend a couple of hours focused on your vision and enter into your calendar the steps you will take.

It needs to feel good and right when you imagine it as real. A vision that feels good has you feeling vulnerable in good way, the kind of vulnerability that shows you are doing something very close to your heart. At the same time, stay grounded in real possibilities. Create a plan that is not too far out, but takes you cleanly out of your comfort zone into the vulnerable land of new experiences.

> "*Most people overestimate what they can do in one year and underestimate what they can do in ten years.*"
>
> Bill Gates

Most of what comes to you in your vision process will fit into the ten-year time frame. Hold that vision as you take the steps to make it real.

For example:

I have a big vision for our Business Academy for Professional Coaches. It includes other coaches leading my programs when we introduce our three certification programs for relationship, spiritual, and business coaches.

I see a community that comes together in person at least once a year, and a year-long leadership mindset program. In this vision I am writing books, giving talks, and producing a popular podcast.

I have created this bigger vision of how I want my business to look in order to help me make inspired choices as I take the teeny-tiny steps forward. It is useful in grounding me as I make leaps of faith. When I fail, it helps me get back on track. When I succeed, I celebrate the vision becoming a reality.

Visions are best when they include what you want for yourself (who you are and who you are becoming), your work (prospering by engaging in your soul-fulfilling livelihood), and the impact you want to have on others (creating your legacy).

There will be iterations of visions for you, as there have been for me. We are always a "work in progress" when traveling on this path.

One of the iterations of a vision I had for my coaching business was when I went back to basics.

At the time, I found that the most appealing vision was a simple structure consisting of twelve ideal clients and three ongoing coaching circles. I wanted to lead a few workshops a year and have an assistant. In addition, it was important that I have open time to write. I also wanted to break into a six-figure income.

I had resisted having this kind of business because it was a little mundane for my tastes, even though it was a leap for me. I have to confess that I had much grander things in my ten-year vision. But, here is the important part—IT FELT GOOD.

As I made it a reality over time, taking the steps and using my vision as a working plan, I realized that despite not aiming for the bigger things in my vision, this iteration included writing a book, speaking to groups, and even going to an interfaith seminary!

So don't forget, it has to *feel* good. The better it feels, the easier it is to make it happen. Now, feeling good does not mean that it will feel comfortable all the time or that fears won't pop up.

Remember, there is a distinction between the fear that comes from the inner saboteur kicking up a fuss because you are heading into new territory and the feeling of "not quite right" when your soul is guiding you to correct your course. Get quiet. Listen to the centered, calm voice inside you. Aim for something truer, even if it seems to contradict what you think you should be going for.

Start With What You Have

"Start with what you have" might sound like a truism you would read on a new age tea bag tag. But it is perhaps the greatest stumbling block in all of creation for us humans.

You can only create from what you have, and you must stand on what you have while envisioning what is yet to come.

When you focus on what you DON'T HAVE and try to create from there, you ignore the gold in your backyard and dig deep, empty holes all over the place.

You need to include ideas and dreams you have for the future. Those that feel good and resonate on a soul level now. In that sense, they are visions and feelings that you "have" now about what we will create in the future.

It's a paradox. To honor what you already have, while holding the growth and expansion you see in the bigger picture of your vision.

The following exercise integrates these two essential elements of a vision. Using the values you have and the experience of honoring them in a way that moves you forward to what is next.

Business Values

One of the most effective and fun ways I know to walk the path of a vision and make it a reality is to tie it to your values. As a coach, you know the connection that comes when you help your clients see the values they are honoring in the important areas of their lives. Applying values to a coaching business works the same way.

One thing that I have discovered in my career as a coach is that there are a variety of types of values. Personal, Relationship and Business seem to be the top three, although I am sure there are more.

While there is a common thread in that values get to the essence as a guide for living your life to the fullest, when you look at a specific area

—in this case, your business—there are distinctions that make the values in that area make sense in a way that a blanket approach misses.

Here is one way to identify a business value:

Unlike personal values that we can experience on our own, business values are specific descriptions of what happens in a business—in the experience of running a business and holding the space of a coaching relationship. They are interactive experiences.

They may evolve a bit over time, but they stay the same in their essence.

It's pretty simple.

Business values are experienced IN the relationship you have with your business and your tribe.

Exercise: Your Business Values

Follow these steps to discover the essential elements of happiness for your work and your business values.

1. Set aside time in a place that relaxes and inspires you. Have a cup of your favorite hot beverage, sit in your

favorite chair, and wear some comfy clothes. Allow yourself to move into a state of relaxed awareness and truth-telling with yourself.

2. Think of all the important areas of work you have experienced in your life. Not just your current ones but past ones as well. You can include those you have been inspired by in books and movies.

3. Begin to identify the interactions in these memories in which your heart opened, your body relaxed, and your mind was thrilled.

4. Look over the list of "starter" words below and then begin to choose your own words that begin to describe the interactions that made you the happiest. (I say "begin" because this is always a work in progress.)

5. Trust your intuition and open your heart to what resonates deeply there.

6. Write down all the words that begin to describe the experiences of fulfillment in the work you have now or have had in the past.

7. You are brainstorming here, so let loose without limits.

8. After a while, you will run out of words. Take a look at the list you have created and begin to organize the words into similar categories.

9. Here you need to be disciplined and truthful with yourself. You need to reduce the list to essential words, word groupings, or phrases that identify your most essential business values.

Business Values Starters
Integrity / Authenticity / Honesty / Fun / Joy / Financial
Abundance / Meaningful Work / Transformation / Well-
Oiled Machine / Effective/ Efficient / User Friendly/
Leadership / Equality / Fairness / Fun / Creative /
Connected / Win-Win / Success

That's a good start. Now, I have one more thing for you to add to your values list before I wrap up this section on Heart and Soul and give you a simple way to write a values-driven story to keep your vision fresh in your mind.

A business has many areas, in and of itself. There is the service or product, of course. And the values of how you want to serve and create impact. These values are usually come to mind first and are much easier to identify than when you put the values lens up to the marketing aspect of your business.

So often coaches bypass this step and include everything in their values list EXCEPT the marketing. It is a thinking error to leave out one of the most important aspects of any business—either completely bypassing it or thinking that is something you can address later.

However when you include marketing into your vision using your values, you get to include that experience as something positive just like the rest of your vision.

Ask yourself these questions to unearth your marketing values:

- Where do you come most alive when sharing your work? What are you doing in those moments?

- When you look at the past, what value was operating when you marketed something successfully?

- What was an unusual way that you wouldn't even consider marketing

- Look underneath for the values.

You might look at the questions above with a fellow coach to make it more fun.

Here are a few of my business values:

1. Have Fun and Get it Done
2. Regular Business Activities
3. An Engaged Community
4. A Compelling Message

Here are a few of my marketing values.

1. The Energy of Love
2. I Always Have Specials
3. Putting on a Show
4. Big Integrity

Once you have explored and discovered around five or six marketing values, you add them to your business values list.

Now it's time to have some fun and put your values into a picture.

There is a connection between the right and left brain when you put words and pictures together. This can be super simple.

Just get some markers or crayons and write down your top 10 business values on a piece of paper in a non-linear way. Then add little squiggles or line drawings, simple pictures that connect you with each of your values and make you smile.

Now the icing on the cake. Here is how to craft your Successful Business Story using those same values.

Exercise: My Successful Business Story

Write the following sentences on a piece of paper and then fill in the blanks.

My vision for my coaching business success is to use my value of_____ to _____.

I get really excited when I imagine the value of _____ and how it impacts people _____ (in particular way).

I attract just the right people by honoring my value of _____.

I am surprised when I see the value of _____ works in my marketing and helps me create the coaching offering I love because _____!

Now you have an inspiring image and empowering story to help you make your vision a reality.

You will also find that this exercise gives you a positive way to project into the future where most of your fear lives. The fear that works to promote feelings of hopelessness, which makes it really tempting to give up on your dreams.

Fear is very sneaky. Even though it may seem positive, *fantasizing* about the future also can be fear-based. Something you do when you can't accept your present circumstances and have those "someday everything is going to be wonderful" thoughts. This can leave you feeling ungrounded and hopeless in the present moment, paralyzing you from taking the action needed.

There is a vastly different kind of future gazing that I call "Dreamland." This is where the Law of Attraction comes in. My

Successful Business Story *is* a manifesting structure that will help you bypass fear and walk down the path of fulfillment.

In addition to My Successful Business Story, you can find a myriad of visioning tools on my website at:

EvolveYourCoachingBusiness.com/exercises.

Nuggets

- It's essential to have a big-picture vision to keep you inspired.

- A vision comes from your soul's wisdom and helps you take the small steps needed to make it a reality.

- The outer signs will show you what is working and what needs to be adjusted. The inner signs help you use your intuition that always lets you know what is right for you.

- Art (Vision) comes before science (Strategic Planning and Action).

- Vision paradox: A vision never follows your desired time-line and may look nothing like you imagined. Yet, when it manifests, it resonates exactly as you knew it would at exactly the right time.

- A vision holds the energy of your heart and soul. Keep it close by.

- In the vision world all is neat; in the world of experience, it can be a mess.

- Visions are not just about the future; they include what you have now.

Now that you know the power of a vision and how to create a vision from your heart and soul, we will move onto the stages of a coaching business. As you learn about the four stages, you may want to revisit your vision to make some tweaks that will align your vision more accurately to where you are right now in your business evolution.

Part 2:

BUSINESS EVOLUTION IN FOUR STAGES

One can choose to go back toward safety or forward toward growth. Growth must be chosen again and again, fear must be overcome again and again.
—Abraham Maslow

We only need to look to nature for evidence that growth happens in stages. A mighty oak starts as a sapling. A baby learns to crawl before walking. Growth takes time, nurturing and the right care and conditions. Sometimes growth comes very slowly and sometimes in surprising bursts.

So, as in all of nature, your business will evolve in stages—and like the seasons, I have found there are four distinct stages to a coaching business. This section will help you understand each stage and its importance, and identify where you are right now so you can take the necessary steps as you evolve your coaching business.

The Fairy Tale

Once upon a time, there was a woman who had a mission. She wanted more than anything to serve the world by helping people become their best selves. She was called to become a life coach and was committed to doing honor to this noble profession.

She got the best training in the world, quit her job, and just as she had dreamed, like magic the clients flooded in. She wrote a book that brought her a massive audience, and before she knew it, she was almost as famous as bestselling author and renowned expert on vulnerability, Brené Brown.

This story is true only in a fantasy I had twenty years ago when I started my coaching career. Some of the facts are correct; I did write a book. I did hit that magic six-figure income and have had a great career as a coach. I did have clients and I did live happily ever after!

There was magic for sure, a lot of it, in fact. But it was in equal measure to a lot of hard work, many twists and turns, and plenty of failure. The reality was nothing like the fairy tale.

A couple of years ago, I took time to take stock. I looked at what had worked and examined the unnecessary suffering I had endured because I did a lot of right things in the wrong order.

If there is one thing I want coaches to know, it is this: There are natural stages of growth, and you can't skip them forever. A coaching business evolves and, when you know the natural stages, you can make choices about how and when to evolve your business with confidence.

Another way of understanding the four stages is to think of how we humans evolve through our lives. Very much like we move through childhood, adolescence, adulthood, and being an elder, there are four natural stages of a coaching business.

Knowing these stages will help you grow your business at a sustainable pace, help you overcome the challenge of not knowing what to do, and give you confidence in yourself as CEO of your coaching business.

The four stages are:

Coach in Training, Startup, Sustainable Success, and Legacy.

I have created this stage matrix based on a combination of my own failures and successes and from working with hundreds of coaches.

Like any other type of growth stages, there are also transitions that need to be navigated. Those liminal times of growing pains (when you identify them) will make the transitions much easier to manage and will build trust in knowing your business will have long-term success.

As clear as these stages are, they also mirror evolution, in general, in that there are always exceptions. And you will most likely repeat your business growth by going through the stages multiple times.

Knowledge is power, so they say. Using knowledge to your advantage is a wise use of this power, even though you may not like all the elements of that particular stage.

Public Service Announcement: If you avoid learning what works best and skip over doing what is needed in each stage, then you leave yourself with a weak foundation that eventually makes your business unsustainable.

Just as damaging is the frustration that comes when you feel like you are doing all the right things but they aren't working!

The good news is you can go back and fill in the fundamentals of a missed stage at any time!

Each stage has four areas that I believe are requirements for a thriving and fulfilling coaching business.

Before I dive into my own true coaching journey, let's look at how these stages can work in an ideal world by reviewing "Coach Jen's" story. (Coach Jen is a fictional character comprised of a compilation of my own journey and that of other coaches and those I have helped over the years.)

The Tale of Coach Jen

Stage 1: Coach in Training

Coach Jen was called to the coaching profession because she wanted to have a positive impact in the world. She believed in being well trained in her newfound profession. She enrolled in a coach training program to learn a coaching model, improve her skills, and determine how she might use coaching in her work.

Though she had dreams of doing great things with her coaching, she decided to focus on learning how to coach first. It wasn't easy. At times, it was so challenging she felt like giving up.

She worked with a handful of clients and stayed determined as she practiced and practiced. She still felt coaching was her calling. She learned how to talk about coaching as a profession without feeling self-conscious. She began to experiment with new ways to enroll clients using her coaching skills.

Coach Jen was grateful to her mentor coach who was not only helping her navigate her training and how to stay in tune with her heart, but also giving her a sounding board to look at her future business dream.

She began putting things into place, little by little. A basic website made her feel legitimate and proud of what she stood for.

With that in place, she ventured into the market with a book club offering that attracted a small but enjoyable group to share her coaching know how with.

Coach Jen did not think she would like networking; it seemed too serious for her nature. She was surprised to find that, although she wouldn't necessarily call it FUN, she enjoyed meeting new people and talking about coaching.

When she enrolled her first new client through a networking contact, she vowed to make networking a habit!

Coach Jen began to put more things in place, like systems for online payments and scheduling. Her mentor helped her develop the forms she needed and, by the end of her training, she was feeling like a real professional.

She signed up for a business development course and pretty soon she was exploring niches and learning how to market to the exact people she wanted to work with.

Though at times she felt overwhelmed, she had a vision for doing meaningful work in the world which kept her moving forward. This work honored her values, life purpose, and just plain made her happy!

Then came the dip when she realized that coaching is vulnerable work, and it would take her way outside her comfort zone!

Coach Jen worked with her coach to name and manage the fears that naturally come up when beginning a new endeavor. Fears such as:

- Who am I to coach people?
- How do I make this work?
- Am I any good?
- Will I fail?
- What will people think?
- Can I really call myself a coach?

She also had myriad questions about how to make coaching her life's work, which required a lot of soul searching.

One of the best pieces of advice she got from a seasoned coach during this time was to take time to dream. What a relief to know she didn't have to have it all figured out yet!

She allowed herself to dream big with a twenty-year vision that included everything that made her heart sing. Then she dialed it back to right now. "What needs to happen this month, this week, today?" she asked herself. She saw it was all about learning to take consistent action. Coach Jen was one smart cookie of a coach!

She realized there were going to be unexpected twists and turns ahead as she let go of "I'm a coach in training" and stepped into "I'm a professional coach."

She made a commitment to keep going.

Stage 2: Startup

Things had gone pretty well for Coach Jen during her coach training and the first few months into her new identity as a professional coach. She found she was getting comfortable in this new life. So much so, she was tempted to look for more training opportunities in this craft.

She had enjoyed the little bit of marketing she had done but was resistant to moving past the training phase and to addressing the many things she didn't know.

It turned out to be the most challenging part of her coaching journey so far. She now found herself feeling the ongoing discomfort of conscious incompetence when it came to her business. She even found herself feeling stupid. Not a great feeling for anyone, but especially someone who was usually as confident as Coach Jen.

What she couldn't see clearly at this stage was how long it would take to create a stable foundation. *This stage can take up to three years to complete.* According to research by the International Coaching Federation (ICF), this is when most coaches fail because they do not do the foundational work of building a business or career.

Despite her feelings of discomfort and vulnerability, she recommitted herself to her business. She saw it was going to take time and realized she needed help. So she signed up for a marketing program that felt heart-based.

Through her own experimentation with the marketing activities that had worked and by trying on some new ones suggested by her coach (who also helped her shift her mindset), Coach Jen began learning new tools and ways of thinking that helped her face this challenge head on and begin to move past her resistance to this phase of business.

She learned having a niche was important whether she planned to be a solo entrepreneur, an executive coach, or join an organization. As her career path, she chose a niche of working with women leaders.

She set up systems to support her marketing efforts, including a simple blog, a basic email list builder and a process for onboarding new clients. She even hired a virtual assistant to work a few hours a month. Coach Jen got help with her bookkeeping and other things that had felt overwhelming.

It took time, money, and effort but after the first year Coach Jen was beginning to see the results of her hard work and tenacity, and believe it or not, she was having fun! She enjoyed being her own boss, working with her wonderful clients, and seeing her own creative self-expression in her business activities.

Coach Jen could now see why this stage was so important. All of the things that are foundational to a business take time. Many of the startup elements cost money and can bring up resistance.

The other big thing she learned during this stage was to balance her time and energy between increasing her income and building her business foundation. She even got a part-time job to ease the financial concerns she had. This step was inspired by a guest speaker at an ICF meeting. The speaker said that many successful coaches started their coaching business while continuing to work at their "day job" or getting a new part-time job.

The speaker suggested options, ranging from working for an organization that uses your coaching skills to something totally different like being an outdoor adventure coach. This prompted a participant to tell her story of going to work for REI in order to experience something very different in her week. She spoke of how important it is to keep a flow of income and stay engaged out in the world!

Coach Jen saw why it is essential to work with a business coach or enroll in a business building program. She was proud of herself because she had done this even when she thought she couldn't afford to. The truth is, she couldn't afford NOT to!

After she really got going, Coach Jen found that being in startup mode can be exciting but also overwhelming when she didn't stay grounded in her own soul's wisdom.

It took courage and a willingness to be publicly vulnerable. To put herself out there. Side benefit....it required that she grow into her best self.

Then, on top of all of the "business" activities, Coach Jen was wise enough to carve out time and resources to enhance her self-care and spiritual practices.

Let's pause here and take this in. YOU are the most important element of your coaching business foundation. The way you feel, the thoughts you think and the energy you put out into the world make ALL the difference.

Coach Jen was able to face the fears that often arise from a commitment to coaching as a career, such as:

- Can I make this work?
- What if I don't?
- What will I have to learn, spend, face, and let go of now that I've committed to coaching as my career?
- Am I ready?
- And on and on and on (believe me).

She learned that the best advice for new coaches is don't fall into the trap of isolating yourself, don't overwork or think that you have to do it alone, and realize no one can avoid failure. Learn to make mistakes; embrace your failures as your greatest teachers. Remember that you are not alone and hold it all as lightly as possible. Remember, this is your dream. It's essential to laugh and play!

Coach Jen was on her way. Her dream was becoming a reality! She decided to add group coaching to her business offerings. She was pleased to learn this was one of the best ways to grow her business, and she loved it! She found having a clear niche and the foundational work she had done helped her easily market a group program.

Coach Jen was now beginning to think of herself as a CEO!

She joined a mastermind group specifically for coaches in business to have extra support and community.

In her mastermind group, they explored great questions such as:

- What's my vision for my business and life?
- What is the impact I want to have in the world?

- Do I want my own business or to work for others?
- What is my commitment to the coaching business?

She often heard the leader tell her:
Don't rush this. Take the next best step and it will come together in time.

Then came the moment when Coach Jen realized she had a business foundation underneath her. She was looking at her calendar one Monday morning and she saw that she had a steady stream of consultations that week. She checked her bank account and sure enough her income had stabilized. She sure as heck celebrated that moment! It was a big deal!

She did a happy dance…

And then she knew it was time to raise prices and get ready to take another leap in the marketplace!

Stage 3: Sustainable Success

Coach Jen had been in business now for almost three years. She had worked hard and enjoyed the journey. She had learned what worked for her and what didn't when it came to running her business. She loved the clients she worked with! Most of all, she enjoyed having steady income that was sustainable as a result of her consistently effective marketing activities.

Jen had diversified her offerings so they were now what was often referred to as scalable, a combination of individual and group programs.

One of her greatest joys over these three years of startup had been developing her own brand with a message she was passionate about! When she realized she could bring her message to the world, all the fricken' work she had done to refine her niche paid off big time!

For Coach Jen, whose niche was leaders she encouraged and repeated a message about owning your feminine power at work and at home.

She had grown in the area of CEO. She now had a few good systems and marketing activities that resulted in a steady stream of consultations. What once had seemed foreign to her, things like sales strategy, now had a very different connotation. She now saw that a sales strategy is just a way to let people know how she can help them. That was the goal after all!

She had basic internet marketing skills, enough to be able to hire the right people to help her. One of her mentors had taught her this valuable lesson. You can't get help with something unless you have basic knowledge yourself. Otherwise, you will be spending money foolishly.

She was also beginning to grow her own tribe! People were following her on social media and signed up for her blog. Now things were really getting fun!

She did things that just a couple years earlier would have seemed like they belonged on Mars. Things like building a sales website. She got help with this, but she did the copywriting herself and took great pride in how the site grew her mailing list. She had some great partnerships and alliances with other coaches, as well as with people who were complementary to her business. She was a big believer in win-win!

Her favorite way to engage with the marketplace was to have contests and give away prizes. She had fun quizzes and other free offerings that helped her target audience solve their problems. She was even able to host live events a couple times a year, which was great fun and always created a buzz for her business.

A couple years into this phase of her business she started a Facebook group and hired another coach to help deliver her programs, which were now popular enough to warrant bringing on more help.

She had a super virtual assistant and a few consultants she could call on to help with specific projects that she cooked up to grow her business. Sometimes these projects were just for the joy of putting something new out in the world.

One thing Coach Jen adhered to throughout this phase, as she had all along, was to make sure she got support. She took courses, joined programs, and hired coaches depending on what felt right for her at the time.

She continued to take marketing and business-building courses. She now loved these as much as her personal growth training, which she took to add something to her business and other times just to feed her soul. With a six-figure income, she could now afford to do these things. Yes...that was a big "YAY" moment for her, indeed!

She was no longer hiding out in those personal growth classes, looking like she was being productive but really procrastinating. In fact, she found creative ways to integrate the personal growth work with the business-building work that kept both her personal life and business flowing.

By year five, Coach Jen was doing some really fun things. She had a signature program she was known for, and which could be delivered online. She learned this was called an "evergreen program," an offering that would be continually relevant and stay fresh for her target audience over a long period of time. At first, not familiar with this business term, Coach Jen made up that it meant a way of selling a program that would lead to her business being "forever green," with that green money coming in. This is very accurate!

Coach Jen expanded her love of writing and performing to include not just her blog, but regular speaking gigs. Ones that put her and her message in front of her ideal clients.

She published articles, hosted a radio show, and finally found her true love with a popular YouTube show that was the perfect way for Coach Jen to get the messages most dear to her heart out to the world. A message, that of course, tied into her business. She had put out a couple of eBooks and now was ready to publish a full-length book!

Despite all the positive momentum and growth she was experiencing, and even though she loved the group work and the individual client work that was so essential to her heart and bottom line, Coach Jen began to feel overwhelmed. At times, her schedule just seemed TOO full. Even though it was full of things she loved.

That happens, right?

One winter day, she had a wakeup call: Her joy for the work had disappeared.

Coach Jen had continued to work with a great coach herself. Her coach helped her to see she had gone a little lopsided with her focus on building her business. It was now time to rebalance and take care of her health, schedule open time, and to put time and attention into her personal life!

Coach Jen began cultivating new habits that helped her take self-care up a notch, just as she had her business. Habits that were nourishing for her whole self: body, mind, heart, and soul.

With the addition of self-care and making time for herself, Coach Jen's business was in really good shape. Even so, and because she is human, she still had doubts.

Fears would sneak up on her. They sounded like:

- Will it last?
- Is it real?

- When is the other shoe going to drop?
- Will people discover that I'm really an imposter?

On the flip side, there was also a voice that whispered:
- Is this really what I want?
- Is this all there is?

When she took time for introspection, Coach Jen realized that she had higher expectations of herself. She was ready to go to higher ground to learn to be authentically confident and comfortable in her own skin in a way she never had before.

It was at this point that Coach Jen took some leadership training to up her inner game. She found a coaching circle that held her to a high standard but still allowed her to let her hair down in order to stay grounded and relax a little!

She was eight years into her coaching career and was at a crossroads. It was a transition point that she had longed for. She was living her life's purpose and channeling that through her coaching business. She had sustainable success which included a good income and a growing business.

However, at this crossroads was also a question. Did she want to create something that would live long after her life was over?

Big ass question for sure!

This question wouldn't leave her alone.

She wondered:
- Is there something I haven't done?
- Do I long for more?
- Am I willing to do what it takes to take another leap?

In this transitional phase, she made the choice to take the leap! Not all coaches choose this path. Some may not even feel the pull or decide that it's not for them. For her though, there was something more and she was willing to enter unknown territory once again.

She wanted to focus on becoming a thought leader and growing her own tribe around her teaching and philosophy. This would mean letting go of things that had become comfortable as well as things that just didn't work anymore.

Then something funny dawned on her. To go to the next phase of her business, the Legacy phase, in a way she had to go back to Startup!

Stage 4: Legacy

Coach Jen did some soul searching to get herself ready for this leap. It was her intention to be an influencer that others turned to for guidance and inspiration.

Yep...that was a leap, all right!

She imagined what it would be like to be a thought leader who was valued for what she stood for. To have many people follow her, join her community, feel inspired, and know that she cared about helping them in ways that were most important to their core values. This became her crusade.

Her core beliefs aligned with theirs. The people she was attracting to her community felt seen and known by her. They were grateful she had pursued her career and was now delivering her message in ways that supported them in learning and growing, enabling them to fulfill their own dreams.

To make this a true legacy project, Coach Jen developed unique intellectual property with her own content, ways of delivering her services, and a variety of products.

She found ways to create those evergreen products she liked so much that allowed her to help people at a lower cost, which aligned with her values. She also had great fun coming up with some high-end offers for those who were committed to going all the way.

She had something for everyone which made Coach Jen happy! Slowly but surely, she began to find her ground in this new phase of her business and life.

She was a thought leader and the figurehead of her business!

Things that had once seemed like a dream were now becoming reality. Her first book was a hit with her tribe. She hosted a wildly popular live event that was sold out!

To help her navigate these waters, she had a top-notch coach who was willing to call her on her "stuff" and cheered her through the ups and downs of this dream.

Coach Jen also had a team working for her.

The day-to-day running of the business was handled by others so she could focus on her leadership. Much to her delight, she found she only needed to play-in where her voice, creativity, and expertise were needed!

She now had time to create, be visible in the world, and have the impact she always wanted! But this didn't mean she was immune to hiccups and an occasional fears surfacing.

Just as she was hitting her stride, Coach Jen took a dip. She discovered some hidden doubts and limited thinking about herself.

She found the "I'm an imposter" fears grabbing her. Who was she to have this kind of success? What if people found out who she really was?

Some of it was just her own saboteurs getting all kicked up and loud. It was also coming from other people.

People who thought she was "way too full of herself, too visible, too ego driven," and all the other negative opinions that can be directed at someone who is on top of their game.

Coach Jen had always enjoyed being a likeable person. But in this phase, she found there were people who didn't like what she was doing because she was now outspoken and original. She was saying things she felt were true but not necessarily popular, which were bound to bring criticism. At times it seemed personal. At times it WAS personal!

As great as this new level of success was, Coach Jen found that, as in her startup phase and anytime she had gone to a new level, she had to consider new ways to stay grounded and in her happy place. It became even more important to her to stay connected to her soul at this stage.

Here are the things Coach Jen learned that really helped her continue to grow as a thought leader.

- It can be lonely at the top, so make sure you don't isolate yourself.

- Address your "Upper Limit Problems" head on.

- To do this well, you will need help from a specialized coach, mentor, or spiritual guide.

- Taking nourishing retreats is not a luxury, it is a requirement.

- Set aside weekly, monthly, and quarterly time away from everything to reassess, restore, and connect with your soul.

- Take lots of vacation time, at least three two-week vacations a year.

- Deepen your excellent self-care habits. Movement and exercise; sleeping; eating; meditating; mindfulness of your health needs; family and friend time; spiritual retreats; downtime; goofy fun time.

- Spend time in nature as much as possible.

- Cultivate your love of music, art, reading, writing, playing, praying, creating, and whatever else floats your boat in this area of life.

- Practice spiritual activities you enjoy and that connect you to a higher realm...and do them often. That is great advice for a coach in any phase.

With her newfound connection to her soul, Coach Jen wrote a new book that was her personal memoir, revealing her struggles as well as her triumphs. She created a new program — the one she had always wanted to build! It wasn't the most popular of her creations, but she could afford to do it simply because she wanted to.

She was speaking to larger audiences and finding it was vulnerable but so fulfilling to have an impact on more people.

She was considering a Ted Talk and possibly starting her own mastermind group with other high-level thought leaders. To her amusement, and at times horror, she found there were some paradoxes in this stage!

It was no longer all about the money, yet she was aiming for a high six-figure income and beyond. To do what she really wanted to do, she realized that she may need to take a dip in income to accomplish this.

Naturally, her vision for her business had changed over the years. Many of the things she imagined all those years ago when she was a coach in training came true. Others she let go of and moved on to create a business that was aligned with her soul while succeeding in the marketplace.

Now her vision had shifted once again. She found herself contemplating things such as:

- What would it take to have the optimal work/play lifestyle?

- Was there a mentor who had walked this path who could guide her?

- Was this the time to give back by mentoring others who were right behind her?

- Was there another way she could give back?

- Did she want to pursue high-level partnerships?

- What was the ideal workspace for her to access her highest self?

Coach Jen was very mindful of the transitions in this stage (there seemed to be many) and she hit a wall at many points. However, what kept her grounded was staying focused on the aspects of her work that brought the most joy. She let go of the rest.

Speaking of letting go, she even reached a point where she wondered if she wanted to let go of her business altogether and sell it to someone who had a passion for leading their tribe!

She looked at her life and business like a blank piece of paper. Did she want to go back to school? Begin training in something new? Start another type of business? Or possibly retire and discover what that meant for her?

Then she came back to two of the most important questions:

- What brought her the most joy in this phase?

- What made it worthwhile to face the challenges and questions that sometimes kept her up at night?

The answer was she now had the money to live freely.

She was having an impact on others in a way she had always dreamed of. She saw that it took a high level of consciousness and intentional responsibility to keep moving in the direction of her heart.

She realized that, inch by inch, step by step kept her moving on her journey, no matter what stage of business she was in.

She was reminded over and over that the most important thing was to stay tuned into the impact she wanted to have in the world and the experiences that brought her the most joy.

When she was able to keep bringing those two things together— no matter what stage her coaching business was in—she was at peace with herself and living a fulfilling and prosperous life.

There is no such thing as perfection!

I would love to tell you that all you have to do is follow in Coach Jen's footsteps and success will be yours. In her story, there is a combination of fantasy and truth. The truth is, following the natural stages of business evolution will help you make good choices.

The fantasy is, you will follow the exact steps Coach Jen did. Reality is you will more likely be much like me, with successes and failures repeated many times over.

What I want you to take from Coach Jen's story and integrate into your business growth is that making better choices than the ones I made in my ignorance will serve you well. Knowing the stages of business evolution, you have a guideline to assess your choices. I wish this had been available to me.

The other fantasy is believing there is any one path that will work for YOU!

There is no perfect marketing plan or person who can show you the way unless you stay true to yourself. There is no perfect path or shortcut to fulfillment in business success.

There is no magic bullet. The magic is taking these stages into consideration as you grow and evolve your business. Your business that matters to you and to those you are here to help.

This is why I wrote a whole book on the topic! On the following pages you will learn all the aspects needed to succeed in business, while at the same time staying true to your own vision and desire to have a full life.

Shiny Objects Syndrome – S.O.S.

Now, let's look at what a true-life coaching business story looks like from a real person...me! This story is a bit like life — it's a stream of consciousness of my path and told through the lens of the four stages.

Stage 1: Coach in Training / Stage 2: Startup

Like Coach Jen, I had a passion for coaching right from the start. I dove into my training. Having experienced a startup business before, I was pretty smart at knowing how to build a foundation my first year.

Stage 3: Moved too fast into Sustainable Success

I went off the rails with an error in my thinking. I moved too fast into what I thought was a sustainable business. I hadn't built the systems and consistent marketing that was needed.

Oops! I found myself in a deep nose dive, going from a consistent roster of ten clients and a yummy team coaching contract to just a few clients, which was not enough to pay the bills.

Back to Stage 2: Startup!

I needed to do more work in the startup phase, so I did. This was an important message for me to learn.

I landed a super fun gig working for a successful coach as her executive assistant, which led to helping upgrade her business. That led to creating an offer for other coaches to upgrade their businesses and a couple of partnerships with other coaches. I was also hired by the Coaches Training Institute to teach their business development program.

As a part of my training, I was enrolled in an excellent business-building program where I learned tons of stuff I still use to this day. Some of these things are included in this book! I had the support I needed, and I put some important systems in place.

My business was back on the right track!

As great as my business background and training had been, you would think I would walk a straight and joyous line to a prosperous business.

No such luck. My niche, entrepreneurs who wanted to upgrade their businesses, was going really well for me. Why didn't I stick with it and grow it full out?

There is an expression "chasing shiny objects syndrome." Well, I fell into that trap and I once again ventured into a phase of business before I was ready! Oh yes, it hurts even now to think about how I couldn't see what was really working for me.

During my business training, I decided to add a new niche to my offerings. Yikes!

(Thank goodness I kept my niche of helping people succeed in small, heart-based businesses, which was paying the bills and aligned with my passion and expertise.)

I added in the niche of couples engaged to be married. I had taken tons of classes and training courses, read books, and as you will read in the story My Hard Lesson, I had a lot of experience in what worked and didn't work in romantic relationships.

My exuberance took over! I loved this niche so much that I once again veered off the trusted path of business building in stages. I wrote a book and created a card deck for this niche. I had a program for couples and even for churches! I went all out without the foundation beneath it.

I had a few clients that I loved working with, and I did deliver my program to a couple churches. But I didn't do my due diligence in discovering what my niche wanted, and my business once again took a nosedive.

It was not a total failure, but it simply didn't have what it took to grow. So, I went back to what was working—my niche of entrepreneurs! Mostly coaches, since those were the people I was best at helping.

Still, there was something missing. During a business development course, the leader teacher guided me to explore a niche in the relationship arena—single entrepreneurial women looking for a soulmate.

This combined my niches in a lovely way. A new niche was born. This time I did ALL the work required in startup and was excited to become sustainable.

Stage 3: Sustainable Success, in and out and in and out and finally IN

I started my own networking group, which was a huge success and gave me the ideal opportunity to reach my niche. I did talks on relationships at my church and was almost there when... again the shiny objects!

I got this idea that I would like to have a radio show, so I applied at the local AM station. It would cost money until I could get sponsors, but I had faith and jumped in with both feet.

The show was a blast, and it did bring in business. I even got to interview some of my heroes like Gay and Kathlyn Hendricks! I did live coaching on the air (how fun is that?), and I delivered my message to many.

My business, however, was not ready for this added amount of time, energy, and money. It was unsustainable and so it had to go. Boo hoo...if only I had known then what I know now.

It took time and a financial crisis (that had nothing to do with my business) to point me in the right direction this time.

I had to have a good income and I was determined to make my coaching business work for the long haul. I dug in once again and this time I made it through the startup and into the sustainable phase of business!

Right about this time I also began leading the certification program for the Coaches Training Institute and realized how much I loved this profession. I wanted to help coaches succeed in business as I had done myself.

I added in a new coaching circle for women coaches, and it was a huge success. I wrote a little book for my niche of entrepreneurial women looking for a soulmate and created a program and course to help grow my business, and it did!

Stage 4 Legacy...or so I thought

I wish I could tell you that I had learned my lesson about the shiny objects. But here they were again. I had a successful blog at the time, yet my itch for the radio show experience just wouldn't leave me alone. I started an internet radio show with some friends and again put a lot of time and energy into it.

This show attracted a REAL internet radio station that offered me a show which included having my own coach and help with marketing to sponsors. I learned a ton from hosting this show! I learned how to speak on the radio, how to conduct an interview, and how to be a thought leader delivering a message. It was unbelievably valuable to me in that way.

But...it brought me NO new business. Luckily, my business was doing really well. My book and program, the coaching circle for women leaders, all sustained my business for many, many years.

Then, you guessed it, once again I veered off the path. Though I enrolled in a seminary to become an interfaith minister, that was not the veer. I found seminary exactly what my soul had been searching for.

The veer was chasing that shiny object again. This time it was creating a program and writing a book focused on the spiritual realm and tied to the relationship part of my work as well. Once again, I jumped in with both feet to what I now see was my desired legacy phase.

I did all the things I had been taught to do by the marketing gurus I was listening to at the time. Go BIG they said. A book, a speaking tour, and a big program were the tickets to success.

I can't say I totally regret any of it! That's the funny thing with shiny objects. Sometimes they can be really fun and definitely a growth experience.

I just wish the penny had dropped a little earlier for me. If it had, I would have looked at what already was working, places where I was already succeeding. Seeing how I could expand, grow the systems, take those step-by-step actions that would move me into the realm where a legacy business would have the necessary foundation to succeed.

I wrote and published a book of which I am enormously proud. It is a good book with a much-needed message.

I graduated from seminary and lined up speaking gigs close by and in other parts of the country where I had connections. I arranged for book signings and created a workshop based on the book. I even considered starting my own church. I enjoyed the whole shebang, I must say. I loved speaking to those congregations!

But for some reason, once I had been doing it for about a year, I realized it was not what I had imagined. Something was missing for me. Were the marketing gurus wrong? I was following their guidance to a "T", but it just wasn't working for me.

I am happy to say that I did get back on track again!

One day, I had an epiphany that allowed me to see that what made me happy was the work that had always been there—working with entrepreneurs, specifically heart-based businesses, more specifically, coaches.

I could go back and do some of the startup work needed for this phase, build the next level of systems to make this iteration of my business sustainable, and set my sights on the Legacy phase with all I needed underneath me to make that leap!

Now I saw that this was the direction I wanted to grow in. At the same time, I stopped to look at my journey.

Where had I succeeded? What had been the true failures? What had I been missing as I zigzagged my way from success to chasing shiny objects and then back on track?

I got very curious about this and made it my mission to figure it out. Now that I had gotten clear that coaches were my niche, I wanted to be able to use my own experience to help them avoid the pitfalls I had encountered.

During a marketing event, I was introduced to the concept of business stages. I felt something dawning. I saw there was something to seeing business in natural periods of development.

At the same time, I saw that these business stages were not an exact match for a coaching business, and solidified my knowing that a coaching business has some real similarities to other businesses.

There are proven strategies that work in any business. I also saw that a coaching business is unique for so many reasons.

The type of people who tend to be coaches are often deeply passionate about helping others. The offerings people want from coaches are very personal and vulnerable. The way marketing works for coaching businesses is in some ways quite different because the relationship has to be considered. Yet, at the same time, those services need to be put into the marketplace in a way that is understandable to the public.

I took my time with this exploration, looking at my own business and those of my clients, and interviewing friends and colleagues to understand the natural stages of a coaching business.

The Four Stages of a Coaching Business were revealed!

I found a clear path that when followed would bring success to any coach willing to put in the time, money, and effort.

That said, I also saw there are many exceptions to the rules. There are coaches who do succeed by skipping stages. There are many variations of what I have laid out here that often include some zigzagging that is beneficial.

There is no such thing as a straight and clear path to success. Knowing the rules will help you make choices about what to do next with more clarity. It will also help you know what the risks are if you choose to zig, *and* how to zag back on the path to your soul-driven success. Essentially, how to manage those shiny objects!

Stage 4: Legacy...for REAL this time

I found that I had to go back and fill in the gaps with systems and structures from the startup phase. Then I could move forward by taking the steps I knew worked from the sustainable success stage. I could now aim at a Legacy Business with the foundation solidly in place.

To wrap up this section and give you a cheat sheet to take with you, I have grouped the nuggets for each stage of business. A big part of the magic of the stages is knowing which stage you are in! So I highly recommend that you take time to explore the linked e-book and quiz. Go to webpage EvolveYourCoachingBusiness.com/exercises and download "4 Stages eBook" "4 Stages Quiz".

Nuggets

Nuggets for Stage 1: Coach in Training

- Enroll in a coach training program to learn a coaching model, improve your skills, and determine how you might use coaching in your work.

- Focus on learning how to coach.

- Work with clients to practice coaching and see if this is your calling.

- Learn how to talk about coaching as a profession. Experiment with your client enrollment style and using coaching skills as sales skills.

- During your training, income is secondary to learning.

- Put in place basic business systems to track hours, schedule clients, and receive payments. Develop basic contracts, designed agreements, and enrollment forms.

- Hire a mentor coach to help you navigate your training and to experience excellent coaching.

Nuggets for Stage 2: Startup

- This is the hardest, though most essential, stage of all. The most important thing to know about this stage is that you need to stay in it until you create a stable foundation on which you can build sustainable success.

- This stage can take up to three years to complete. According to research by ICF, this is when most coaches fail because they do not do the foundational work needed to build a business or career.

- The first thing to do in this stage is to choose a niche. This is important whether you plan to be a solo entrepreneur, executive coach, or join an organization.

- Narrowing your area of focus is what will make it possible to communicate with the marketplace easily. Instead of throwing spaghetti on the wall, aim at a clear target of your ideal client.

Nuggets for Stage 3: Sustainable Success

- You will know you are fully in this stage when your income is steady due to consistently effective marketing activities.

- You may enter and exit this stage, or maybe you want to stay here for years. Some coaches stay here forever.

- Create a recognizable brand with a central message, look, feel, and voice.

- Put good systems in place so your marketing produces a steady stream of consultations.

Nuggets for Stage 4: Legacy

- You are now an influencer that others turn to for guidance and inspiration.

- In this stage, you are a thought leader who is valued for what you stand for.

- The people who follow you are inspired and feel you care about helping them in ways that are most important to their core values.

- Your core beliefs align with those of your tribe. They feel seen and known by you. They are grateful you have pursued your career and are delivering your message in ways that support them in learning and growing, so they too can fulfill their dreams.

- You develop unique intellectual property including content, services, and products.

- You have a team working with you to keep the marketing fresh and the everyday workings of a business humming.

- You have your own coach and mentors who are there when you face challenges and to guide you into the unknown territory of this exciting stage of business.

- You have open time in your calendar to plan and prepare as well as to take the essential time OFF to recharge your creative batteries.

One of my lessons in life and in business is that we can't always see our own journey clearly. It can be helpful to have some insight that gets to the truth of the matter.

To that end, I have a handy dandy e-book and super fun quiz to help you determine where you are on your journey and provide you with actions that can support you in stretching into that stage and moving forward. Go to webpage EvolveYourCoachingBusiness. com/exercises and download "4 Stages eBook" "4 Stages Quiz".

Closing Nuggets

- Knowing your stage of business gives you a map that will guide the growth of your business.

- When you pinpoint your location on the map, the next step for you will reveal itself with ease.

- Your journey through the stages is unique and your path may look quite different than ones I have described.

- There is no "wrong way" to use this map.

- All "mistakes" are opportunities to learn and grow. Many are incredibly valuable to make.

Take these nuggets and resources with you on the journey to building *your* coaching business. They will help you remember which step is next and when the time is right to take that step. Use the steps in the order I presented them or in a way that best serves your vision. But remember, if you veer off the course, you can always review the steps and do the work to create that solid foundation. Do the heart work to find your vision and create your own fairy tale ending. Don't be afraid to imagine sustainable success and watch out for those shiny objects that may get in your way.

In the next section we will delve into marketing. The why, the how, the when, and the how much. I'll share marketing tools, skills, advice and my personal experiences. I also share wisdom from other coaches and my trusted mentors.

It's time for you to learn how to market *your* business so you can achieve the kind of success and financial security that nourishes your bank account and feeds your heart and soul!

Part 3:

MARKETING YOUR WAY

Stop Selling, Start Helping.
—Zig Ziglar

*Business Opportunities are like buses, there's always
another one coming.*
—Richard Branson

People generally agree that marketing is necessary to build a business. But with a personal enterprise such as coaching, one that is centered on YOU and how you can help another person, marketing (aka asking for money) can seem wrong somehow. Even out of integrity.

Just the opposite is true. Marketing your coaching business is 100% integrous. This activity that someone coined as "marketing" is simply letting people know how you can help them. The secret to good marketing in this business, however, is to do it your way. People want to know you are authentic and that you care. They also need to hear what you have to offer in a clear and concise manner so they can make an informed choice.

In this section, I have woven in proven marketing strategies with ways to find YOUR way of marketing. I start with one of my very first successes!

Unconventional Wisdom

I was almost done with my coach certification program, when it hit me: If I were really going to make a go of this coaching thing, create a new career and all, I would need to up my marketing game.

Up to this point, I was gaining clients primarily through word of mouth. A lot of that effort was using MY mouth actually. I told everyone I knew about coaching and was not shy in asking if they were interested in learning more. No one was safe.

Since entrepreneurs were my niche, I hit up:

- The woman who owned my favorite bookstore
- My hairdresser
- My brother-in-law
- Even my husband!

I realized I needed to look beyond this small circle, so I began reading marketing books. I found they mostly left me wanting to gag. They were so dry and didactic. I was still working for the Postal Service at this time, and I had enough of the dry and didactic on a regular basis.

I wanted to create success in my own business in a different way.

However, I also knew from my work with the Postal Service that rules and structure certainly had their merits and that there are some basic rules that should always be applied. I hung my hat on the one, pretty simple rule of marketing that applies to any business—I needed to reach more people.

With that one rule in place, I allowed myself to get creative. To brainstorm and dream of ways to reach more people that might be fun and effective.

I hit on this one wacky idea. I called it my Front Porch Marketing Plan.

It was spring and I was studying for my coach certification exams, spending many hours reviewing my notes and reading from my coaching book and other types of materials.

At the time, I lived in Gettysburg, PA, and my house was a big, white colonial with pillars and a charming window in the front. It had the most beautiful front porch. Like so many people in town, I had admired this house for a long time. It was on a well-worn street, along the path between my little town and the local YMCA where everyone took their kids to lessons, enjoyed exercise classes, and much more. I loved this special house for two decades before buying it.

This tree-lined thoroughfare was also a great little street to walk down. Anyone who lived in town or nearby pretty much had to go past my house to get to the YMCA. Many people choose this street to take a stroll, especially on beautiful spring days.

The plan was this: I would study outside. Either at the table on the porch or on the steps leading to the porch. While in the happy state of soaking up all the learning that I loved so much, I would attract people who were walking by. I might even get the attention of folks who were driving by.

Simple plan with a clear outcome: study outside and reach more people.

As I had hoped, many people stopped and talked to me. They asked what I was doing. I told them. Some were interested in finding out more.

When my yoga teacher stopped to chat on her way to work, I was thrilled to share my new career with her. She was so excited that she told me I could promote my coaching after every class! There were other good conversations and connections made that first week of the Front Porch Marketing Plan. I was on to something!

But it was in the middle of week two that the stunner came.

I was studying on the steps one morning when a woman came up to me. She looked familiar but I didn't know why. As she approached, I put my workbook down to give her my attention.

She had a flyer in her hand. She told me about a 5K race being held in a few weeks. She went on to explain a bit and then introduced herself as the director of the YMCA. Of course! My son worked there, and this was his boss.

She was well known in our town and very influential. I found myself getting a little shy and quickly took the flyer and thanked her.

Instead of moving on, she got curious about what I was studying. Hmmm...funny how when you put something out there it comes true!

I overcame my shyness just a bit and told her what I was doing. My passion kicked in and we had a really good conversation about how coaching works. She had never heard of it before.

Then she looked me straight in the eyes and said, "This sounds exactly like what I have been looking for. I have a team I work with at the Y, and I think we could all use some individual coaching as well as group coaching."

Say what? Was she offering me a coaching gig? I was too stunned to reply in the way I would have liked (calm, cool, collected, professional). I blathered something and we made vague plans to connect and move forward.

The story doesn't end here. You know those times when you are so intentional? When one good thing you do leads to another? It is like you have opened a magic doorway that keeps leading you forward to more opportunities. I believe these are the times you are 100% Soul Driven. When you are aligned with your values and higher purpose.

My soul was aligned with my purpose. This was then supported by proven strategies that gave structure and clarity to my purpose.

In this case, it was a simple marketing strategy—reach more people. Use my talent for engaging people in conversation. Use my skill of listening to hear what is important to them. Simple but powerful when we are soul driven.

So here is what happened. That very day, just an hour or so later, as I was about to go inside for lunch, an acquaintance walked by and stopped to chat. We had a lovely conversation during which I told her about my new coaching career.

She told me that, coincidently (and she herself felt the synchronicity of this) she was starting a new kind of networking group THAT VERY EVENING. She thought it would be the perfect place for me to promote my business.

I must admit that at this point I felt the tingle of manifesting in reality what had been in my imagination. It conjured up excitement and oh, shit! What am I going to say? Am I ready? All sorts of gremlin voices took over.

That evening I was still nervous, but my excitement led me to this woman's house. She introduced me and told everyone I was a life coach. At one point, she asked me to speak to the whole group. Holy Moly! NO, I thought.

But out of my mouth came a story about therapy being like looking in the rear-view mirror at the past while coaching was about looking out the windshield at where you wanted to go. I must have read that somewhere! It worked well enough to get some interest from the group and one or two women asked for a sample session. I was happy!

Then, as I was getting ready to leave, feeling the night had been a marketing success, another woman approached me. It was none other than the director of the YMCA. The same woman who had been on my porch that morning talking to me about coaching her and her team.

She said she was more excited about my coaching after hearing me talk. Could I meet at her office *the next day* to talk more? Yes, I could. Yes, this marketing stuff really works. My way.

I did meet her at her office, and she offered me a contract that included individual coaching with her and each of her team members as well as group coaching to be implemented later.

This was beyond what I had ever imagined could happen with my simple plan!

When I break it down, I see My Front Porch Plan has all the components that can work for anyone. For example:

- I had a clear outcome in mind. I aimed for using a proven strategy for growing any business: reach more people.

- I knew my strengths, and I used them. The location and attraction of my house, my engaging personality, and my skills of listening and hearing what is important to people.

- I was intentional in implementing this plan.

- I faced my own vulnerabilities.
- I moved forward despite the gremlins yammering away.
- It was unconventional. I did it my way! I am a wacky person. I believe in the law of attraction. I believed in what I was offering with all my heart.

The I Hate Marketing Myth

I would be rich beyond belief if I had a dollar for every time I heard a coach say, "I hate marketing."

This phrase has come out of the mouths of many of the students I teach at the Co-Active Training Institute, a lot of coaches who approach me for help with their businesses and, more often than you might imagine, coaches who are successful and have been at this a long time.

The sentiment is surprising to me, and I don't think it's true. It is one of those blanket statements that covers a lot of ground and, in doing so, misses the main point.

Marketing, as I illustrated with my unconventional wisdom experience and at its most basic, is simply letting people know what you do.

Where the HATE comes in, I believe, is in not understanding this, and a few other simple things I am going to lay out here.

So, we will use the coaching skill of *making distinctions* to break this down and uncover the different parts of marketing.

Let's look at a simple list of the three main parts of marketing:

- Let people know what you offer.
- Find out who they are, what they want, and what they long for.
- Discover how to meet them where they are and let them know the benefits of coaching.

A big aspect is helping people see that what you offer is valuable to them. **This is where the HATE often comes into play.**

Coaches collapse the valuable part. What stirs up the saboteur crap for sure is thinking that marketing is *about them and their own personal value,* or *even the value of their particular coaching.*

It's not about you—the point of marketing is to find the value you offer other people and what they will get from coaching. Can you see this is a very different perspective from which to view marketing? Can you FEEL the difference?

You let people know what you offer and how it could benefit them. Then you find out if it would be helpful to them. This can seem scary, I know. This is the part of marketing that is heading into a sales conversation.

It can start to seem slimy, and you might find yourself wanting to convince people that coaching is the next best thing to sliced bread. That icky, needy feeling might creep in. Will they like this? Will I be rejected?

"I HATE MARKETING" often arises at this moment and you want to go running for the hills.

Am I right?

What is really called for at this moment is for you to simply be a coach!

Find out what people need, what excites them, what makes them tick, their dreams, and the obstacles they face.

And very importantly, do not let yourself become attached to whether the person would find your coaching of value or not.

It may not be for them. You don't need to coerce or convince them.

Try not to be attached to making a sale. Be more interested in deepening the relationship to find out if the two of you are a fit. Scary? Yes, it is. But not something to HATE, in my opinion.

(This is where the stages of business work is really important. If you have income from another source (for example, your day job or a new part-time job), then that will help you come into these conversations with potential clients with an air of calm and not a feeling of panic.)

There is an arrogance and danger in thinking you don't have to learn your own way of marketing. In thinking that the strategies of marketing don't apply to you or your coaching business.

Of course, you increase your chances for success 1000 times over when you put yourself in the path of the people who are looking for YOU, for what only you have to offer.

That's called a niche, and it's oh so important.

The Cool Thing About Niches

When I decided to become a life coach and make it my career, I realized it was an alternative path, especially compared to working on an executive team for the Postal Service. It required taking off the golden handcuffs that provided all kinds of financial security but kept me trapped in a job I didn't love.

I made some major changes in my life to prepare for this leap. I sold my house and bought a beautiful, old house that had been turned into five apartments. The rent from four of the apartments paid the mortgage, and it was a great location to have a home office where I could see clients. This is the house that also had that wonderful front porch!

I made a deal with myself that I wouldn't quit my job until I had ten paying clients and a successful marketing plan. That gave me some hustle because I really wanted to quit my job, but it still took about a year to make this happen.

I had learned about marketing, enough to make and follow a basic plan, and I had learned about the importance of a niche from my experience in being in fruit business with my first husband.

As you know, the niche I chose in the beginning was solo entrepreneurs who were looking to grow their businesses. I was pretty successful with this niche. My own circle of friends (and fun strategies like My Front Porch Plan) generated a stream of inquiries and helped maintain my ten-client goal. That was pretty cool, and sold me on the concept of niches.

My first clients ranged from massage therapists to small contractors to yoga teachers and a woman opening a gift shop that featured unique crafts.

Although having a niche was a proven and conventional marketing strategy, I did not abandon my own unique way of navigating the world.

I made my niche choices based on practical and personal things such as:
- I chose a niche that had an easily identifiable problem.
- I chose a niche that was willing to pay for my services.
- I chose a niche that was easy to talk about.
- I chose a niche that I could easily reach via my extended group of friends and other networking paths.
- I had credibility with this niche because of my work with the Postal Service.

Most importantly, my niche had to light me up. So...
- I chose a niche for which I had personal passion

During this time my first marriage fell apart and I moved from my small-town safe haven to the big city of Los Angeles. My old networking ties were broken, and I had to rebuild my business.

In my new city, I connected with a lot of life coaches. I realized that many were also solo entrepreneurs with the same problems I had addressed as a business owner myself.

This was at the point when I chose the niche of life coaches and other personal growth professionals, and I did a lot of networking! I networked at events hosted for the sole purpose of connecting and networking, at personal growth trainings, and even found it effective to network at a few coach-specific events.

My very first client was pretty prominent in the coaching world. She was way ahead of me in terms of business success. I found this didn't matter because I had learned the basic problems to address, and I knew I could help her solve them.

Just that one client and her eventual testimonial was a huge help in restarting my business in a new city.

Adding to my previous lessons:

- It is helpful to go outside of your own realm of relationships to meet new people.

- Even highly successful people will pay attention if you can address their problems and give them hope.

- How to leverage that one testimonial into a new stream of clients.

I will never forget when one of my first coaching clients from this new stream reported she had achieved her financial goal through our work together. I then realized she was making more money than I was!

If you're tracking from my story in Section 2, this is when I felt drawn to add another niche to my work. I believe it is fine to have more than one niche, as long as you first succeed in one before expanding to another.

I was in the middle of my divorce and I wanted to help other women NOT make the mistakes I had made. As my marriage came to an end, I could clearly see where I had made bad choices.

It seemed to me that if couples could address the issues (of which I was now quite aware) *before* they got married, it would help them make better choices.

I got so excited about my niche I wrote a book called *It's Not Just a Wedding, It's Your Life!*

I also created a "Staying Engaged" card deck to help couples communicate about some of the more important but vulnerable topics they need to explore together.

My business was called "The Queen of Hearts Wedding Coaching." My logo was a very clever queen of hearts playing card.

I thought I covered all the bases with this niche. I knew the problem and I had the solution in spades!

I also knew where to find these people. One such place was a wedding show.

So, I signed up for my first wedding show. Oh, you would have been impressed with my booth! It was beautiful, with my books and cards stacked in the middle.

The only trouble was, all the brides avoided it like the plague.

After a while I became desperate. I went onto the showroom floor and tried to lure people with my pretty little deck of cards. As soon as I told them what I did, they practically RAN away.

The only interest I had was from mothers of the brides-to-be. They told me they thought what I was doing was great but their daughters were more interested in saying "YES to the Dress" than having deep conversations with their honeys.

I held onto this second niche for many years.

The most lucrative part was working with couples or other types of partners who had issues. Their problems were clear, I had the solution, and they were willing to pay for my services. I found this rewarding on some levels, but it was not in my wheelhouse!

You can be GOOD at something but it is not in your wheelhouse if it drains your energy. This means it is not sustainable over time and there is something else that will be better for you and your business success. This is often true in a coaching business.

Start with the easiest niche and then refine as you become clearer on what area of a person's life or with what circumstance you most enjoy helping people.

When deciding on your niche, remember to:

- Do the research, even if you think you know what the answers will be (because I didn't know).

- Read the feedback from the marketplace, even if you don't like what it's telling you (I didn't).

- Be willing to switch your niche if it's not working (took me a long time).

- Pay attention to what's in your wheelhouse. I built a successful business solving a problem that wasn't in my wheelhouse. (You will find an exercise that will help you identify what I call your Genius Wheelhouse in Part 7.)

During this time, I was still focusing on the entrepreneur niche. I found a wonderful job teaching a business development course for The Coaches Training Institute where I learned a ton and connected with other coaches, some of whom became clients.

I also took a couple of relationship coach training sessions. During a marketing course in one of those programs, the teacher stressed the importance of making sure that your niche was looking for your solution.

That's when the penny dropped.

When he talked of niches to avoid, he used the example of offering relationship coaching to engaged couples. I am not kidding! Ouch!

During this training, I took the time to look at what had been successful in my coaching work. It was pretty obvious that the number one niche for me was entrepreneurs.

I still wanted to expand my niche and include relationship work, so this time I went to my niche of entrepreneurs to find out what relationship problems they wanted solved.

That's when I created my new niche of "successful single entrepreneurial women looking for a soul mate." They had the money and motivation to do the work and pay me for my services.

They were already in my network, too. Many of my current and past clients, colleagues, and friends were in this niche. I could easily speak to the problem, and I simply reworked all my relationship coaching exercises to focus on helping single women.

I wrote a little book called *The Art and Science of Romance*, which led to a tele-class and eventually to my Women's Alchemy Coaching Circle, which helped me grow my business for over a decade.

From there, I wrote a new curriculum aimed at those in the niche who consider themselves leaders. I call it "Leaders in Love."

I loved that niche, and it was the one that brought me a sustainable, successful business for many years.

When working your niche:

- Iterate your niche until you hit the intersection of what you love doing and what the marketplace wants to pay you to do. This is the sweet spot!

- Repurpose what you already have, to bring it into alignment with what people know they want.

- If a niche is working, keep working it!

Hang Out Your Shingle

One of my business mentors explained a niche to me this way: Your niche is the front door of your business. Above the door, you hang a shingle that lets people know what they can purchase in your store.

It's a front door that a clearly defined group of people see and want to walk through because it speaks specifically to their problems, needs, and desires. This is where a niche comes in.

There is also a back door to your business.

The people who enter your back door come from referrals, people you meet who resonate with you, a person who hears you speak or someone who reads a blog you wrote and wants to work with you.

They may not even really know what you do or care what your niche is. They are strongly attracted to you or have heard such great things about you that they are interested in your services.

You will want to have those back door clients!

This solves the problem some coaches have when they face choosing a niche. They don't want to turn people away. The good news about back door clients is that if you love them, you can always work with them regardless of your niche.

That said, most sustainable businesses need to have customers consistently coming through the front door.

I say most because there is always the exception to the rule. I believe it is much wiser, however, to follow this rule and create a niche so you have a front door for your business. This is the number one rule that has worked for me and the coaches I have worked with who have prosperous businesses.

Discovering your ideal niche can feel daunting because there are so many ways to slice and dice a niche. It could be based on a specific profession, a circumstance in life, on gender, age, or geo-graphical location, or an area of life like relationships or business, and on and on.

It could be that your expertise, education, or affiliations define your ideal niche.

A niche includes one or more of the following:

- Area in which you have expertise
- The problem/dream you most want to help people with
- An area of life you are passionate about
- Their story matches your story
- They are easy to reach
- They have specific qualities you like
- They are segmented by age, gender, race, profession, sexual orientation, etc.

Now it's time to play! Look at your options. Begin to explore the different types of niches and find the type you would like to focus on. Landing on a niche is part art and part science, so you need to give yourself time to experiment.

One client I worked with identified her niche by looking at what she really wanted to help people with, which was their finances. She brought in her own life story of anxiety around money and how she overcame this. She chose a demographic based on race and gender.

Another client looked at people in her profession that were in her network. She knew their problems well. She chose to work with these professionals as they were preparing to leave medical school and enter the job market. They were easy to find.

One simple way to discover your niche is using the who, what, why structure.

- "Who" is the description of a group of people. Who are your people?

- "What" is the problem you can help that group of people solve. Name one.

- "Why" is the benefit from working with you. Think of a specific result this group of people would have once you helped them solve that problem.

With this three-step structure, you can play with iterations of potential niches. You might start with the tangible benefits they will receive. Then work backward to find what problem would most likely need solving and then what group of people might have that problem.

If this structure doesn't float your boat, not to worry. At the end of the chapter, you will find many other processes to explore your niche.

In my experience playing with a niche is an ongoing process.

In order to make sure your marketing plan comes from the heart, choose a niche you love.

Then, it is simply a matter of iterating your way through the various stages of business growth with that love leading the way.

These next two stories, which come from different times in my life and different types of businesses, shine a light on successes and failures along the way to learning how powerful having a niche can be.

You can have the most wonderful marketing plans in the world, but if you don't have an audience who wants what you are offering, then marketing will become something you hate because it will not work or it will be a slog.

As you read these stories, I encourage you to soft focus and let the storyline take your imagination wherever it wants to go. You don't have to make a direct connection to your business, but instead take in the essence of the experience each business had.

The Little Store that Could...Have

I have always had an entrepreneurial spirit. From the time I was a little girl, I loved to experiment with selling things in the marketplace.

I put on plays and charged the neighbors to watch. I sold cookies and lemonade on hot summer days. There was something so compelling to me about using my own creativity and effort to make people happy and, at the same time, to put some money in my pocket!

My first business venture as an adult (twenty four years old to be exact), however, taught me a lot about using my creativity and effort in a way that *did not pay off*.

I learned the hard way about the basic rules of business, and it's a lesson I have never forgotten.

At the time, I was a young mother living in Gettysburg and everyone I knew was having babies! One of the problems I knew for myself and heard from my friends was how expensive baby clothes and equipment were and how quickly babies outgrew both.

I attended a nearly new baby goods sale at the YWCA and was shocked to see a long line waiting to get in. An idea blossomed in my mind at that moment. Wouldn't it be fun to have a nearly new children's store?

I had a great network of friends who could contribute, and I loved the idea of repurposing beautiful and useful things.

I was so enthusiastic about this idea that I started asking for opinions of everyone I knew. The venture was met with a lot of positive support, so I decided to go for it.

Just as I made this choice, one of the best locations in town became available for rent. In a small town, this was a rarity. I jumped on it and quickly began setting up shop.

I set up a consignment system for friends and the general public. I planned for my own acquisitions by scouting yard sales.

I also had the idea to add homemade things, such as toys, quilts, and clothing. My neighbor made wooden rocking horses and cradles. They were works of art! He agreed to selling them at the shop and I adorned my store window with a beautiful rocking horse along with the best nearly new items the store had to offer.

My store seemed to be bound for success right from opening day! Mothers flocked in and were happy with the selection and prices.

I couldn't keep the rocking horses and cradles in stock. As soon as one went in the window, it sold. I had a similar experience with the handmade goods. People were hungry for unique gifts for baby showers, newborn baby presents, birthdays, and Christmas gifts.

This was great news for me because these were the most expensive things I sold, and I made the most money on these items.

I would love to tell you I succeeded in this business. The truth is I closed down after just six months!

It wasn't because I wasn't selling things. The problem was I was not paying attention to WHAT was making me money! I had an idea that my niche would be young mothers, like myself, looking for nice things for their kids at affordable prices.

With that myopic view, I totally missed the more lucrative niche. These were the family and friends of people with babies who were looking for unique and special gifts.

This niche was filled with people who had money they were eager to spend!

Instead of doubling down on the handmade items and finding more craftspeople who wanted to sell their wares, I kept my focus on the hand-me-down items that, although they were selling, were bringing in little revenue.

If I had been more aware and savvier, I could easily have made a niche switch and started to focus more on providing handmade gifts for children, and perhaps even expanded that to include other areas of life.

It makes me cringe even now, because the store that took over kept all of my furnishings. For over twenty years, that store looked exactly as I left it.

And, yes, you guessed it, they sold handmade wares.

Lessons learned from the "Little Store That Could...Have"

- I chose a niche that had a problem, but they were not necessarily interested in paying a lot to have that problem solved. Let this one sink in for a moment.

- Since I had to make a profit, my items were more expensive than going to a yard sale or getting hand-me-downs from family and friends.

- I hadn't considered how little I would make on each item and how much work the logistics were for that type of business.

- I totally missed a really good niche!

- If I had done my research or paid attention to what people really wanted, the ending of this story would have been much happier.

- The niche that was eager to be served (let's call it family and friends of babies and young children) had a problem. They could not find a unique gift for the endless baby occasions of family members and friends...baby showers, births, birthdays, christenings, etc.

- Perhaps another problem of this niche eager to be served was they didn't know how to become the favorite grandparent!

- I might have expanded my niche to other types of people or occasions where there was a problem finding a special gift.

- I might have come to the awareness that in this small town of 8000 people, there were over a million tourists each year! I am certain I could have tapped into this niche and discovered a related problem around gifts, don't you think??? The most successful store in Gettysburg did just that. They are not only a thriving business serving people in the town with their unique handmade items and other super cool and unique items, but tourists flock there every day. When these tourists return home, they or their friends want to purchase additional unique items! Several years ago, this business listened to their niche customers and expanded their service to include a fabulous online store.

Here's a side lesson: An important element of success in any business is to be able to track the internal signs as well as external signs when they come together.

A few years before opening my store, I was passionate about weaving and had woven an array of unique wall hangings. I sold several of my weavings in gift stores at prices that amazed me.

I even had my own art show, with an opening and everything, at Gettysburg College.

I gave up on the idea of weaving as my work, but I realized it had not given up on me. My weaving passion was expressing itself through the beautiful crafts I put in my store that had been selling so well!

We all have those deep longings of our soul's purpose that continue to knock on the doors of our awareness asking to be expressed in the world.

Low-Hanging Fruit

One of my great inspirations on how amazing it is to have an accurate niche—and the benefits of doing some research on your niche—comes from my experience in the fruit growing business!

My first husband, Eddie, and his three partners, began their journey in the fruit business by buying an apple, a peach, and a pear orchard. They thought it was cool, going back to the land and doing something far out...very different from what their strait-laced upbringings and college educations had taught them about work.

This attitude is much like that of many life coaches. We chose our profession because it is full of life and far away from the mainstream business environment. The connection between fruit growing and coaching isn't as far-fetched as it might seem!

When they first started their business, Eddie and his partners followed the path of other fruit growers in our area—selling their fruit at a roadside fruit stand and to food processors.

What they found was a territory that was well worn and in which it was hard to make much of a living. It also didn't give them the opportunity to grow spectacular fruit using very few chemicals, which was what jazzed them the most.

A few years, marriages, and a combined total of seven "babies on board" later, they were forced to rethink their marketing plan, which was barely keeping shoes on the kids' feet and food on the tables.

That's when things got interesting.

Eddie and his partners brainstormed ways they could branch out, and they came up with the idea that maybe people would like to have fruit delivered to their door. This seemed like fun, so they bought a van and started a delivery service.

A great idea, perhaps, but it turned out that people were not interested in this service. People didn't mind driving to select their own fruit at one of the many fruit stands in the area. They actually preferred that to home delivery.

More brainstorming ensued and the partners had the idea of finding a niche for their business. The niche they chose was "wealthy people in the city who valued fresh food."

It seemed logical that, unlike less wealthy people, these people would be interested in paying a premium price to have quality fresh fruit delivered to their door.

One of the partners, Jim, just happened to know a lot of people in the nearby city of Washington, DC, and he thought they would be interested in homegrown fruit.

This time, with the sting of failure still fresh and a clearly identified niche to engage, it made sense to **do some market research before putting a lot of time and money into marketing to their new niche.**

Jim went door to door in some of the wealthy neighborhoods of his friends, asking people what would interest them when it came to having fresh fruit delivered to their homes.

They told him two things:

1. They were very interested in his product. They were health conscious and liked the idea of having the best-tasting fruit. They also really liked the idea of knowing the people who grew their food.

2. They were not at all interested in home delivery! What they wanted was community. They wanted a place in their own neighborhood where they could gather together and purchase homegrown food.

Farmer's markets were just beginning to take off at the time. They were mostly in very public places with a lot of competition among the farmers. They were also highly regulated, which limited the potential profit that could be made.

This particular niche liked the idea of a farmer's market, but they wanted one that was more boutique and that they could call their own.

With that knowledge the partners began brainstorming how they could best serve their niche customers.

Eddie and I decided to take a drive to DC during that time. While we were there, we took a little tour of one of the wealthy neighborhoods Jim had visited. We noticed there was a beautiful church with a large parking lot.

An idea flashed in my mind. Churches primarily only use their parking lots on Sundays.

A church parking lot would be a perfect place for a little farmer's market! This particular church parking lot was lovely and right in the middle of the neighborhood where Jim had been knocking on doors.

In my opinion, it took courage for Eddie to approach that church with this kind of off-beat idea. He felt vulnerable, like we all do when striking out into a new marketplace.

At one point, he just decided to do it. He walked through the church door and, as providence would have it, the minister was there preparing for his Sunday service. That started the ball rolling!

After some conversation with the minister and later with the church's board of trustees, the answer was a resounding YES.

A little farmer's market in the parking lot would provide the church with some income and, even more important to them, it would bring people in the neighborhood right to their doorstep and create good will in the community.

From day one, the niche-based farmer's market was a success. There was no competition, and they were able to provide their "tribe" with exactly what they wanted. A unique experience of community, access to healthy, homegrown food, and a connection to the people who grew their food.

This all started in the early 90s and, from that one little market, their business grew to include dozens of similar markets. On any given day of the week, you could see one or more of their trucks heading to DC, loaded with fruit and other fresh grown food.

They were able to sustain this success for over twenty five years, developing their business, expanding their product line, and growing some of the best fruit in the region while providing a healthy income to the four partners and their families.

Takeaways for your business:

- The four partners wanted to do something special to increase their income and align with their passion for selling amazing fruit.

- They started with a dream and decided on a solution without doing any market research to find out if anyone actually wanted that solution. They wasted time and money.

- They didn't give up. They learned from this lesson and regrouped.

- Then they chose a potential niche. They knew their niche people could afford the higher-end product that the partners most wanted to grow and sell.

- They did their market research. They asked the vulnerable questions.

- They brainstormed over and over again, iterating their ideas until they landed on something their niche wanted.

- They identified a clear point of pain (lack of connection to neighbors) and a dream (healthy fruit and a connection to the growers) for which they had a solution.

Now that you know the WHY of having a niche and stories to fan the flames, I have some pointers that will help you claim your niche. .

Your People Need You!

Now you are ready to really dial into your niche. This aspect of marketing can take you from good to great! It can supercharge your marketing plan, besides, it's fun!

Perhaps you will discover a new niche. A group of people you just love who will love you back because they feel that you get them.

Maybe you will find a niche that has been right in front of you, but you never saw it before. People you can relate to, or maybe folks who are quite different from you but pull at your heartstrings and light up your passion to have impact.

If you have doubts, I suggest you suspend them at least enough to read the following chapters. Let go of thoughts you might have had about the limits of having a niche and embrace the possibilities that await you.

Learn the big Why of having a niche that aligns with your own wisdom of how we humans work.

A niche is that specific group of people who will benefit most from what you offer. You need to know your niche so you can invite them into your business! Just as important is the fact that your niche needs YOU!

The Sweet Spot

Helping people identify their niche is my superpower, and I am excited to explore it with you on the following pages!

There are a few things I want to underline before I go any further.

As life coaches, we know that it is not our job to solve problems for our clients. It's our job to help our clients solve their own problems!

The rub is that the promise of an authentic solution to a problem someone identifies is what motivates them to reach into their pocket and purchase a service. Many times, they hope *someone else* will solve it for them.

The promise we make to our niche is that, through coaching, they will have a transformational experience in which they will learn to solve their own problems and realize their unique dreams.

Here's why having a niche is so important. We need to know specifically who we are talking to in order to connect our heart to theirs. When we describe "problems" in our marketing copy, we do it in a way that lets our niche know that we understand what they are experiencing, that we have been through our own tough times, faced and overcame challenges, even if ours were in a totally different area of life, and that we can coach **them** to overcome the obstacles **in their own way**.

This creates credibility and trust in us and what we offer.

Having a clear niche is essential for easy, successful, and joyful marketing of a service or product.

Easy…because it provides a framework for your specific message, a simple and powerful way to connect with people by being able to speak directly to their pain and their dreams.

Successful…because when you speak credibly and clearly to your tribe about a concern close to their hearts, they will hire you to coach them or join your group or program to uncover ways they can solve their problem.

Joyful…because if you really do the work to find an ideal niche for you and your business, the fulfillment of your promise to that niche will be in your wheelhouse.

That is the Sweet Spot—when you find you are focused on helping the people you most want to help and they are happy to pay you for such a valuable service.

The challenges that may arise with marketing and selling are much easier to overcome when the end result is making money by utilizing your strengths to help people get not only what they need but what they WANT—and are willing to pay for.

Whenever something I am offering lands like a thud in the marketplace, I am sure it is because I haven't hit on what people really want. Don't fret if you too have made this mistake.

When I was moving out of the startup stage and had one foot in sustainable success, I sought support from a business coach. He specialized in helping coaches and had great tips that worked wonders.

I will never forget how he encouraged me to put a simple structure to use.

(I believe the official word for this kind of thing is a "Niche Statement.")

This particular niche statement format started with "Do you know when_____?" or "Do you or someone you know_____?" Then, of course, you fill in the blank. I used the latter to take my coach's suggestion out for a whirl. What came out of my mouth surprised even me, and my coach loved it!

So, I got brave and let myself be vulnerable. At my next opportunity, I stood in front of a networking group of women entrepreneurs and asked, "Do you or someone you know have a love life that is in the toilet?"

I swear, those are not words I ever use!

To my astonishment, when I looked out at the women in the room, almost everyone had raised their hands.

They were smiling, too. As if to say, well of course, that is something that happens to everyone. I also saw painful recognition on a couple of faces.

After the meeting, I was approached by several women who were curious to find out more about what I did and if I could help them.

That was the pay off and the lesson learned. A niche statement that has a seemingly rote structure, and even using words I don't usually use, helped me connect with these women. It let them know there was hope, and it brought me business.

Below is a fun exercise that will help you connect with your people in a way they can understand. When talking to people about your business, it can help you articulate what you most want to convey when you use some of these types of techniques. They are simply a way of wording things that makes it easy for the human mind to understand.

Niche Exercises

Here are a few simple exercises that you can use to play around with your niche statement so you can clearly tell people what you offer them. This is the key: When you put your focus over there on the people you most want to help, talking about your services becomes easy.

Here is a way to create a niche statement:
- Do you or someone you know....
- Name a problem.
- Well, what I do is...
- Name how you can help them solve this problem and the what the end result will be.

Here is another way using the Who, What, Why matrix:
- "Who" is the description of a group of people.
- "What" is the problem you can help that group of people solve or the dream you can help them will realize.
- "Why" is the benefit to them when they work with you.

Example:
(**Who**) I work with life coaches who (**What**) have a desire to succeed in business using proven business strategies aligned

with their soul's wisdom (**Why**) so they have a prosperous, lifelong career.

Here is another structure I learned from Marisa Murgatroyd:

Do you know when…
Describe a moment in your ideal client's life when they are faced with the situation/ problem you've identified as the one they need your help to address.

Well, what I do is…
Identify the solution you offer.

So that…
Identify the transformation/results that happen because of what you do.
Or

Do you know when…
Name the dream the people in your niche are yearning to make real.

Well, what I do is…
Identify how you will help them make that dream come true.

So that…
Identify their experience of living the dream.

Here's an example:
Do you know when…
Professional coaches are really passionate about the work

they do, but they hit a wall when it comes to growing their business?

Well, what I do is…
Help them create a successful business that fulfills their soul's purpose.

So that…
They no longer worry about what they don't know and start having fun doing the work they love that's changing the world.

Go to webpage EvolveYourCoachingBusiness.com/exercises and download "the Top Six Niches for Professional Coaches".

Using proven strategies and unconventional practices that align with your own wisdom aimed at a niche you are passionate about is a big part of this success map laid out in this book.

Now, we are going to add another destination to your marketing map.

A Message that Matters

So there I was, in the oh-so-important startup stage AND having just moved to the sprawling city of Los Angeles. I had to reach more people—my people. So I went to a networking meeting held in a fancy hotel in Santa Monica. It was far, far away from my Midwestern roots and the East Coast small town where I had lived all of my adult life.

I was in awe of the place and the people. How would I ever stand out here, I wondered. Then it got worse. As the women at each table stood to do their 30-second pitches, I heard, "I am a coach" more times than I ever imagined I would.

The question *How would I ever stand out in this crowd?* just got louder!

One woman announced that her expertise was helping people craft a message about their business. Perfect!

Soon after the networking meeting, we met at her office. When she talked to me about how a good pitch works, and it sounded right up my alley. I knew how to deliver an inspiring message and how to talk about new possibilities for people.

Then she told me something that almost brought me to tears.

In order to really have an impact and stand out, even in a 30-second pitch, I would need to tell the vulnerable truth. To reveal my own weaknesses or failings.

The resistance was visceral. A great big NO, not that!

I had worked so friggin" hard to look good, for God's sake. People were actually listening to me and believing I could help them. Did I really want to show them all my warts? I took a deep breath and gathered my courage. I tried it out, right there during our first session, standing in her office.

I told a vulnerable truth about my first marriage. How it had failed due to my own ignorance and selling out on my own wisdom. Not just once but over and over for years. I felt the heartbreak and pain as I told this story.

My coach was moved to tears. She told me my story had impacted her personally. Darn…there was no going back now. I had to come out from behind a curtain where I had been comfortable talking about coaching, and now include my own pain and growth in my marketing message.

As time went on and I became more comfortable speaking about my own stuff, I had a moment of great joy.

It came to me while standing in front of a room full of people at another networking meeting. I was talking about what I learned when my first marriage ended and how I now brought that insight to help others in my role as a coach. I realized my "marketing message" was actually one of hope.

What I heard and FELT from people in the audience was that they were grateful to hear my message because it broke through their shame and gave them a new perspective on their own life journey. They felt known and seen. Some had similar experiences and it normalized their own story. Some had experiences that were nothing like mine; however, they too had sold out on themselves.

Crafting a message to help you reach the marketplace is more than a sales technique. I would even go so far as to say it is NOT a sales technique at all. It just so happens that speaking authentically and telling our stories in a way that names the pain and brings light to the solution is a gift you can offer the world. And that will attract the right people to you and your business.

To have the impact you really want to have, you will want to create a message that matters. A message that is yours to bring, to give people hope, or to kick them in the ass. A message that is at the heart of your WHY for being a coach.

This message comes from your own experiences. Winston Churchill famously said, "Never let a good crisis go to waste." This is exactly true here! Sharing your own stories, especially the vulnerable ones, makes good use of your failures, foibles and when you triumphed over great odds.

When you add a message onto your marketing map it will make everything easier and, yes...more fun!

Over the twenty years I have had a coaching business, my message has evolved. As my niche has shifted, I have used different stories to connect with my tribe.

I have never had trouble finding those vulnerable truths! I have plenty of experience with failure, making mistakes, doing stupid things, and doing things unconsciously even though I have a high value for consciousness.

Humbling but true.

The biggest challenge I had was in taking those true stories and crafting a message that made sense as a marketing message yet stayed true to my quest for telling the vulnerable truth.

I took a variety of marketing, writing, and business-building courses and eventually created my own templates and structures to create a message I care about, and more importantly that resonates with the people I most want to help.

It has become one of my favorite aspects of having a coaching business. Being able to reach more people than just my clients. To deliver a message that helps people and gives them hope and inspires them!

Your stories are central to the message you want to deliver in your marketing.

Your message matters to the people who share your beliefs or have been in similar situations and are looking for inspiration to lift them up.

We all have stories to tell.

When I first started my coach training, I was so enamored with coaching that I was totally obnoxious about it! I told everyone I knew how great coaching was. There came a point that even my good friends started to tune out.

What I found as I progressed in getting the word out is the message that people most wanted to hear was one that focused on the impact coaching could have on them. People want to listen to the radio station WIIFM (What's in It for Me).

Just as important, though, was the bigger, more inspiring message. What is possible for any and all of us? The possibility of achieving dreams that feel out of reach. The ability to be your most authentic, messy, brilliant, quirky self and have that be a part of your success. The key to a fulfilling life.

I learned the importance of having a message that included my own vulnerable truths during my very first venture into marketing my coaching services.

The Big Ask

Some moments stand the test of time. I believe the memories that stand out the most are those that happen when we are doing something that makes us feel alive. One such moment for me came right after I had finished my first coach training course.

I was on fire with this new profession! Part of that fire came from my own transformation after having attended just one three-day training course. In that course, I learned how to listen to others in a new way. To hear what was really important, to see their essence shining through all the crud that life can paint over the authentic person we are in our soul.

I was also the recipient of that listening—being seen, known, and called forth in a brand-new way.

I was ALL IN and had made the choice to pursue Life Coaching as a career. I didn't have a speck of doubt about this choice. I love when choices are that clear, don't you? It is a rare experience.

In this particular moment, which I remember with absolute clarity, I was in front of my big, old computer, which was sitting on the desk my best friend, Corinne, had made especially for me.

I took in a deep breath and started to write a message to my nearest and dearest. I was announcing this new career path and asking for their help.

I wanted to let them know what I was up to, and I wanted their help in promoting my coaching services to people they knew.

In my memory of this message, I really laid it on thick, espousing the many ways coaching could help people with every problem known to man. How coaching could bring about any dream, help people achieve any goal and reach the highest heights.

It was a bit over the top, I suppose, but I believed it with all my heart. I decided to be vulnerable and just put it out there.

I wrote that message with my heart on my sleeve. I hit send. I waited.

I remember one of my good friends pulling me aside a few days after I sent that message. She felt it was a little embarrassing to have gone so far. Her advice was to tone it down a bit. That is advice I had been receiving my whole life. Something I no longer intended to do. No thanks.

I did realize, though, she had a point. If I were to connect with people and let them know what I did, perhaps I would need to bring the benefits of coaching down to a more relatable level.

I played around with a few results I knew coaching could bring people, and came up with my first flyer.

I put that flyer everywhere!

On the bulletin board at the YMCA. In my acupuncturist's office. I sent out another message to loved ones with the flyer attached.

Then I started to get responses, and some were interested in finding out more!

Hurrah, I was on my way.

From those two messages, sent from a vulnerable and true place, my coaching business was born.

A few of my friends hired me. A few more had referrals. Many cheered me on and asked how they could help.

This effort led to many more efforts during my first year as a coach. As I navigated the land of becoming certified and fought the demons that come with learning something new, I also grew in my experience of marketing.

As my business evolved through the startup phase and into sustainable success, I had the urge to tell a story that was pivotal in my personal and spiritual growth. An experience that had defined me as an adult.

It was also an experience where I learned such a valuable lesson it helped me navigate my life and was central in how I made choices when it came to my business.

This story was that BIG to me. I started by telling the story to inspire people personally and spiritually at my church. My minister asked me to talk about love, and this story had the power of love right at the center. I eventually crafted a sermon based on this story, and it was at the heart of my ordination as a minister.

I understood that telling this story had an impact on people in exactly the way I wanted.

The story is so traumatic and dramatic in nature. For years, I had hesitated to tell anyone other than close friends because I didn't want a point to be lost.

As my life and work evolved, I opened up the circle a little— telling this story to friends and family and even in a sermon made sense to me. Yet it was hugely vulnerable, beyond any other experience of my life, but I could see how it fit into a context when told to these audiences.

To tell it as it connected to my business seemed like a big stretch to me.

The story is about being kidnapped as a teenager.

How could that possibly be related to my coaching business, I wondered?

The urge wouldn't go away, though. I just knew I had to tell this story to my own tribe of coaches. There was a message I wanted to convey that was at the heart of this story. A message about miracles and trusting in yourself, even when the odds are against you.

Once I decided I would take this leap, the perfect opportunity presented itself. I was hosting a retreat for my Women's Alchemy Coaching Circle. I had been wanting to tell them about the shift I had made in my business. To tell them the new structure, but also why I was making a change and why it mattered so much to me. I hoped I could find a way to tell them all this and inspire them to join me in my new venture. Inspire them to also believe in their own miracles and trust in themselves.

So, I sat down and wrote my story. I was surprised at how, once I had made the inner connection from the story to my work, it was easy to make the outer connection to make the points I most wanted to make.

I told the story at this retreat, and I watched as these women I loved were touched. There were tears and laughter and nodding heads as I described the years I had sold out on the very lesson I had learned during this traumatic experience.

At the end, I felt this amazing warmth and connection in the room. The women told me how they had related to my story and were uplifted. They also were excited about my new business venture and wanted to know more about it.

This experience led me to home in on this particular story and to use it often. I was even able to hone it down to its essence in a short story when needed.

I have included both the long and short versions in the next chapter, to give you an example of how a story can be used in your marketing even if it is totally unrelated to your niche or what you do—it's about the impact of hearing about a challenge you faced and how you overcame it.

We all want to know how to face our challenges and how to overcome them, don't we?

The other connecting part is tying it all together in a way that makes sense to the specific people you most want to help. So read my stories and then get ready to start putting your own stories out in the world!

The Story of My Life

Below is the shorter version of my story crafted into a marketing message for my coaching business. Though dramatic, you will see that any story can tie into your business.

On a hot and sticky summer day when I was seventeen, I was walking through a one-horse town in Colorado. I had just left the Sheriff's office, where I had positively identified the man who had kidnapped me the night before.

I was still in shock, but as I was walking in the hot sun, it struck me like a thunderbolt—what I had always believed about the world was true. I had experienced a real miracle.

I had tuned into my soul and felt the support of Spirit and acted from that wisdom… which is what saved my life.

I knew without a doubt at that moment there is a spiritual realm we can connect with at any time to receive guidance.

We can always choose to act from love.

I wanted to shout this to the world and show exactly how people can tap into this realm to create their dreams.

This quest to share what I learned has taken many twists and turns since then…and there was a period where I gave up. The world didn't seem to want to hear about this miracle from me.

Even when I became a life coach and had the opportunity to help people, I defaulted at times to the tried-and-true methods of creation and I held back on bringing what I knew about the power of love.

It was only after I had suffered a big financial loss and realized I needed to increase my income or close my business that I revisited my miracle.

With a new determination and purpose, I finally cracked the code of conscious creation. I was able to use the exact formula I had used to save my life to save my life coaching business.

I called it *the Soul Search* process, and I committed to using it consistently to help grow my business in a way that fulfilled my soul's purpose. Within a year, I had doubled my client base.

Within three years, my husband was able to quit his job and join me in our business.

Now I have a program where I show life coaches how to align their soul's purpose with proven business strategies so they stop worrying about getting clients and start enjoying all aspects of this profession that is changing the world.

Below is a longer version of my story crafted into a marketing message for Soul Driven Success Academy.

I was seventeen and on a road trip with a girlfriend. We were heading to Denver and had stopped at a motel for the night about an hour away. I was in the hotel bar trying to find someone to check us in. I struck up a conversation with a baby-faced cowboy who overheard me talking to the bartender.

He told me he could take us to Denver and we could stay with friends of his. He knew the city well and it would be fun. My gut said no but my head said yes, so a few minutes later, there we were driving with a stranger to pick up some clothes at his sister's house. There were kids playing in the front yard which helped me relax, but the cowboy was in the house for a while and my original gut feeling came back. My girlfriend felt the same way. We decided we would ask him to drop us off at a hotel for the night. When he got back in the car, something was really different. He was no longer chatting us up; he was quiet.

I made the request to be dropped at a hotel. He ignored the request. As we drove down the highway, he passed one exit and then another. I asked again. This time I was feeling afraid, yet I wanted to keep my voice light. He finally took the next exit, but instead of turning towards the bright welcoming lights of the hotel, he turned left and drove into the dark night. There was silence in the car. Then he said, "I want to see those clothes fly." When I looked his way, I saw he was pointing a gun at us. The clothes flew. We drove on into the middle of nowhere. No houses, no lights, no hope.

He turned onto a dirt road and stopped to open a gate into a cow pasture, and then drove some more. In the middle of the middle of nowhere, he stopped the car. As he was putting the car into park, he set the gun down and my girlfriend grabbed it and jumped out of the car. Before I could even register what was happening, the cowboy was out of the car chasing her. I heard gunshots and had no idea who would return. In that little space in time while I was alone in the car, I asked God to help me. I had a flash of my hometown newspaper with a headline: Local girls killed in Colorado. I was just seventeen and I didn't want to die.

I asked God for guidance, and it came. I heard the words. Just be yourself. Do what you are good at. You are really good at being friends.

It may have been a couple of minutes later when the car door opened, and the cowboy and my girlfriend got in. They were both angry. I made my move. I turned to the cowboy and said something about how annoying my girlfriend was. I smiled my best, good-old-girl friendly smile. He ordered her out of the car then. I put on his cowboy hat and turned up the radio and started singing. "I Shot the Sheriff" was playing and I got the irony.

I won't go into all the details of what went on in that car while we were alone, but eventually I talked him into letting my girlfriend back in. I kept up the front of being annoyed with her but now the cowboy was singing a different tune. He was saying he was going to have to kill me even though he really didn't want to. He had killed other girls. He had killed men in Vietnam. It was really no big deal to him.

My friendship skills were growing thin at this point, worn down by a feeling of hopelessness. I kept going, though, giving him reasons to delay the inevitable.

Suggesting that we could continue the party at a hotel was my best shot. This back-and-forth debate of what to do next went on long into the night with us all sitting in that hot car, until I felt another shift when he stopped talking. Once again, I prayed. Again, the answer came. "Love him, Kat. Open your heart and just love him." This was the very last thing I wanted to do. How could I do that? But I did.

I let go of everything, including my plea for my life, and just opened my heart and loved him. It was almost as if in a dream that I realized the car was moving. He opened the gate, and we were on the road again.

He drove to the hotel this time and checked us in.

We all walked into a room and my girlfriend turned to him and told him he would have to leave because she wasn't "that kind of girl." He left with a promise to come back later in the day. I may have even kissed him goodbye before we closed the door, locked and dead bolted it, and called the police.

I picked his picture out of the book of potential suspects and Sheriff Charlie told me he had been praying for this day. The cowboy was suspected of killing a couple of local girls and of raping many others.

They hadn't had enough evidence to put him away...until now. Charlie not only believed my story, but he also believed in me. He thought what I had done was brave and smart.

We left the police station to go find lunch. I had a moment I will never forget. Walking down a dusty street, hot and scared in the midday sun. It was a one-street town with a couple of bars, a movie theatre, and a diner. As we approached the diner, I stopped dead in my tracks in the hot sun and felt a lightning bolt. I no longer felt fear or despair.

I knew that what happened to me had been the greatest gift of all. I had been shown, in no uncertain terms, that what I had believed all my life was true. There was a higher power; I could tune into something greater than myself. When I searched my soul, there was an answer, and love was the most powerful force of all. We always have a choice! With this knowledge rising in me I felt such great joy. Instead of feeling like a victim, I actually felt happy.

When I was seven, I experienced God talking to me. Sitting in a field beside my home, I asked God why so many people were unhappy. That day, I heard that it was my mission in life to help people get what they really wanted, to help people to be happy. To teach people about love.

Now after this terrifying and miraculous night, I had the proof I needed to carry out my mission!

When I looked back on that seven-year-old little girl, I also saw how much my life had changed. At that moment when God spoke to me, I was sitting in my own kingdom.

Not just the castle I had created in the field with blankets, where everything, as far as I could see, belonged to my family. The beautiful house my father had designed was a landmark on the quiet Ohio road where I lived. My grandfather owned all the houses my neighborhood friends lived in. There were acres and acres of fields, trees, and streams that belonged to my family. My parents were teachers and well known in the community for their charitable contributions.

It was a wonderful life.

Fast forward five years and that little girl's life was about to change forever.

When I was twelve, I was asked to give the commencement speech for my church confirmation ceremony in front of a congregation of a thousand people and a radio audience. I was asked to do this, despite, or maybe because of, my passionate participation in the class where I questioned the teachers, the bible, and my religious beliefs.

I remember writing the speech with confidence, even though I had chosen to tone down my rhetoric. I stepped up to the pulpit and spoke with no fear at all. My greatest hope was that my mother would hear my talk on the radio. She was in the hospital with late-stage cancer.

She died early the next morning. I have always believed she went in peace after hearing me speak about my spiritual devotion.

It was a big surprise and it cut me to the core when that church abandoned my family in our greatest time of need. It was the early

70s and my dad was a loving but neglectful parent. He let us run wild and the church folks were scared of the influence we might have on their children.

That probably contributed to my becoming absolutely terrified of ever speaking in public again. Something in me turned off during that time.

Things didn't go well for my family after that. My father lost his job and all his money. He sold our house. There came a time when he didn't have enough money for us to live together as a family. I was homeless. At fifteen, I moved in with my sister and her friends. My sister did her best, but she was just seventeen. There were drug addicts in the house and the partying made it hard for me to keep up with my schoolwork. I was alone with no one taking care of me.

Two years later, my dad regained his financial footing and bought a house for us, but I was lost in more ways than one by then. I managed to graduate from high school and planned to go to a local college. Then I decided to take a trip that summer to Denver with my girlfriend.

After my moment of joy on that dusty street in Colorado, all I wanted to do was to preach it from the rooftops. "God is real! Love is real! You can make a choice to live, no matter what the circumstances. You ALWAYS have a choice." I would love to tell you that is what I did. But the truth is, even after the clarity I had in that moment, I shut down this knowing for a long time.

My girlfriend and I took a Greyhound bus home. My dad didn't know how to face what had happened to me. I delayed college and joined a Quaker community on an apple farm in Pennsylvania. No one wanted to hear my real story of love. They wanted to focus on the drama. It didn't help that Patty Hearst had been kidnapped at the same time and many compared my story to hers.

I was shaken to my core one morning three years later while reading the Gettysburg newspaper that usually focused on PTA meetings and car accidents. Instead, on this day, there was a story that came all the way from Colorado, which featured a cowboy who was in prison for kidnapping a couple of teenage girls.

He had been let out of prison on work release and the story revealed a gruesome picture of how he had gone on a killing rampage that left five dead. The story concluded with a police chase that ended with the self-inflicted death of the man who held me captive all those years ago. I was reminded of how awful that time had been. I was reminded of the truth that was revealed.

My spiritual awakening was threatening to people, and I wanted so badly just to be safe in the world. I wanted to belong again. I had no one to take care of me so I made the choice to tone it down. I wanted a normal life. On the normal path like other people, so I turned away from my spiritual mission.

Instead, I was the life of the party. Always up for a good time.

I married an older man and settled down. We bought a house and had two beautiful children. I felt I just may have achieved my goal.

I never wanted to face that feeling of being alone and homeless again. I went to work for the US Postal Service. I wanted a normal life and I had one. Everything looked good on the outside. What was happening on the inside was a different story.

It was a cold, rainy fall day and I was alone in my house. I was home from work early and the kids were at a birthday party. I was in physical pain, which had been going on for over a year. Even after surgery and a lot of tests, the doctors couldn't figure it out. I started to cry and it was as if a dam burst, and the tears wouldn't stop. I was crying for my mom. I was crying for the little girl who was lost in the world.

I had never really cried about losing my mom before. It had been twenty-one years. I was thirty-three and it was just dawning on me now. The tears really poured when I faced the fact that, after my mom died, I never again had someone take care of me. I felt lost and alone in the world. Even though I now had my own family, a good job, and nice house.

My best friend, Corinne, came when I called. She had never known me to cry before. In pouring out my story to her that day, another fact dawned clear as could be. I had sold out on my spiritual knowing, sold out on who I really was. I had wandered off the path of my heart while seeking a normal life. On that day, I began the process of opening that door once again. I read spiritual books, sought alternative healing methods, and even took a yearlong eastern philosophy training course.

During that time, I healed my body and my soul. One day, in the training course, we were doing a little vignette and they needed someone to play the part of a spiritual teacher. I stood in front of the class playing my part. I never felt so at home in the world. I knew this is what I was meant to do. I opened up the spiritual channel wide.

I had a really good life, though, and I didn't think this would fit in. I was living on the nicest street in town. I had a job many would envy. It paid well and gave me lots of prestige. My husband and I were well respected by our peers, and we had a full social life. I had two amazing teenagers, whom I adored. Yet something was missing. I should have been happy. My husband often told me that. You have everything, Kat, why aren't you happy? You should be happy.

I was sitting in my newly remodeled master bedroom reading the morning paper one Sunday and I saw an article about life coaching. I had that feeling I have come to call "Insane Intuition." I knew this was going to be a part of my career path. It was an alternative path that had been calling to me for many years.

There was a part of me that still wanted to hold onto the normal lifestyle I had worked so hard for. A part of me that wanted to be a mainstream kind of woman. But I wasn't. The alternative path, the one where spirit is my guide and I trust in something beyond the linear world, is where I am genuinely happy. I made the choice to take a big leap in my career and become a life coach. It has been the best choice of my life. Once I surrendered to living my life on my terms and put my hard work in the direction of my true calling, I found that soul satisfaction I had been craving.

I did the work and took the risks it takes to succeed as an entrepreneur. To add to my fulfilment after finding success as a life coach, I became an ordained interfaith minister. During the almost two decades since I left my corporate job and conventional lifestyle, I have experienced one miracle after another. It has also been messy and called for me to continually be true to myself in ways that are often uncomfortable.

I have failed more times than I would like to admit, and I have discovered things about myself that have been hard to face. It is all worth it, though, because I am happy with who I am, what I do, and how I do it. The people who walk beside me and those I lead amaze me each and every day.

One of the big surprises has been how useful everything that has happened to me during my life has been. A string of entrepreneurial pursuits that gave me a love of business that started when I was six with a cotton candy stand. The many failures I experienced that I can now use to help others. The jobs I had on the mainstream path that taught me a lot about how to succeed in business, as well as showing me the things I never would sell out on again.

The story I shared with you today, I realize now, was exactly how it was supposed to be for me, so that I could do the work in the world that spirit has set forth for me to do, way back when I was that scared twelve-year-old girl without a mom.

People who are called to make life coaching their career often have spiritual beliefs, intuition, and a knowing that is not based in linear facts. They usually don't know how to make their strengths work for them in a "day job" and in the world. So they compartmentalize. I believe they succeed in life, but only in certain areas and in limited ways. They are successful, but not happy. They may have joy, but not the soul satisfaction they crave.

The Soul Driven Success Academy gives you the structure to make your dream a reality. The path to be yourself. The support to be successful in your work. The confidence to let go of thinking you need to be accepted by everybody. The tools you need to attract those in your tribe.

The alternative path is messy. A long and winding road that includes facing hard truths and seeing your true worthiness. Succeeding on the alternative path means you may not achieve what your ego wants you to achieve but you may succeed at what actually satisfies you heart and soul.

Are you in a place, like I was, where you know there is something more, but you keep looking at your nice home, bank account, and successful job as a reason to ignore that voice?

Or, perhaps, you feel you do have it all, but you still want more? Maybe while I shared my story about self-sabotage, you realized how you sabotage yourself, and see how that has held you back. And you know that now is the time.

Are you ready to discover *your* way on the alternative path?

If so, I will help you listen to your own inner guidance to create real success in your coaching business. Just like when I tuned in and found spiritual guidance to do something very practical that saved my life, I can help you tune into your own guidance to create the success that makes you happy.

You will learn what I learned so long ago, when I realized what I believed was true. You are a powerful creator. You have magical powers as well as strengths and skills you can put to work for you in practical ways.

The Academy is ideal for those professional coaches who want to have it all! It's not just about making money, it's about how you live your life. Maya Angelo defines success as "Liking who you are, what you do, and how you do it." You will receive the guidance, tools, and support of a tribe you need to be in business on the alternative path. You will create a platform for your business and programs you can use with your own clients.

I'm not promising you will become rich, though you very well might. I'm not promising you will bypass the challenges, though you might find them easier than ever before.

I'm not promising you will be an overnight success, but when you do succeed, I'm promising you will be happy. I will bring you home to yourself and your true calling. You will have a business that feels like home.

It's Time to Tell Your Story

That is how I used my life story to connect with the people I most wanted to help. I didn't see exactly how the dots would connect until I sat down and wrote it out. I did a lot of variations to get to the main elements that I felt were both vulnerable for me and useful for others to hear. The point is, to give people hope and inspiration. If I can do it, so can they. If I can write my story and connect with people, so can you!

Exercise: The Story of Your Life

Below is a simple yet powerful exercise I have done myself and have used often in my work with coaches. It will help you unlock the stories, often bubbling underneath the surface, that will help you understand your own life and be able to share your lessons with others.

Set aside about thirty minutes with paper and pen.

On your paper, write headings that cover the decades of your life. Allow about half a page for each heading.

Start with 0 to 10, then 10 to 20, 20 to 30, and on—up to and including your current decade. Label each with a word that defines that decade (like childhood, teens, twenties, thirties, or just the numbers).

For each decade, write down the moments you remember experiencing strong or deep emotions (joy, gratitude, awe, love, laughter, pride, sadness, anger, fear, etc.)

Pay special attention to YOU.

What you were thinking, what were you feeling, what about this moment stands out, the impact it had on you... your very being as well as the actions it motivated you to take.

Notice the moments:

- When you felt grounded in your power and comfortable in your own skin

- When you felt wounded, ungrounded, and in pain

- Those that, for some unknown reason, have remained memorable

- Those in which you made an important decision with lasting impact

Write down just enough words to identify the memory for yourself. It doesn't need to be a long description (unless it's calling for that). It can be more like a memory prompt that evokes the experience and its meaning for you.

When you are finished, begin to connect the dots to your current work.

What were the most impactful moments of your life that have led you to the work you are most passionate about now?

It could be that what made you angry or was painful is now your crusade.

Maybe your moments of joy alerted you to a special gift or high value of yours.

There may be a clue to something important in a memory that just won't go away, and you can't imagine why it sticks around…but there it is.

Write down your thoughts and insights about the connections between these memories and the business you are passionate to be doing now.

Use this to know yourself better as well as to tell the story of your life to yourself and others.

Nuggets

- Having a niche makes it easy to reach the people you most want to help.

- Identifying your niche is simply knowing who you want to work with, the conversation you want to have with them, and the expected results that conversation will give them.

- Authentic use of these strategies will increase your success.

- Coaching skills are incredibly powerful business-building tools.

- A marketing message is how you inspire others to believe in themselves enough so that they are willing to make a change in their life.

- The best marketing uses your authentic voice in a way that gives inspiration to others.

This section on marketing is in some ways the center of any kind of business success. I have included the proven strategies that are timeless. I also hope you took to heart the MY WAY of taking these strategies and making them your own. In the next chapter, you will discover there are fun ways to market your business. In each of these marketing practices, the main ingredient will be you, and of course those teaching stories and messages that we all learn the most from.

Part 4:

ATTRACT A CROWD

---

*I attract a crowd not because I'm an extrovert or I'm over
the top or I'm oozing with charisma. It's because I care.*
—Gary Vaynerchuk

Looking at the map of your business after having read this far,
what do you see? If you have followed along, you should see that
marketing is simple. You can stop hating it, or if you were already
on board the marketing train, you will have more love! There is a
spot on the map that holds a place for a niche you absolutely love.
A wonderful, sweet spot that brings your passion to the people
who need it most.

Then, there is the crossroads where you take the road less traveled and stay true to yourself and the unconventional ideas you
have. Yet, in your backpack are the proven strategies that work
every time. A beautiful spot on the map contains your message.
The stories you have learned, your greatest lessons, and the wisdom
you have to bring to the world.

Now, you are ready to put your marketing message into the world big time. This is where things get fun. It's time to attract a crowd!

Love for Sale

One day shortly after I first began my coaching business, I was having lunch with an executive who was a big wig in the organization where I worked. We were sitting in a booth eating really bad food trying our best to make it through the day.

He casually asked me if I thought I was going for to apply for a new position that had just opened up.

I told him that actually I was planning to take off the golden handcuffs that had bound me to the Postal Service pretty soon to start my own business. I just couldn't help myself. I was so excited about my new business that I started gushing about it.

I told him what coaching did for people. How I listened and how much I cared and that I just loved my clients.

He turned to me with a bite of fish on his fork and said, "That sounds like another profession, you know, the oldest profession there is. It sounds like you are selling love." I sure didn't like this at the time. It felt like a put down and sexist to boot. But the truth is, our profession is different.

Marketing a coaching business is not like selling nails. As a coach, it is essential that you always come from the heart. In some funny way, what you are selling is LOVE.

You are making a promise to potential clients that you will support what is in their hearts and help them achieve things they couldn't do on their own.

These achievements, the ones people tend to hire a coach for, are based in their hearts not their heads.

It is for this reason that the marketing of a coach business can have a positive impact on others while building your business.

You must be vulnerable and speak from your heart while you are getting the message out about what you offer and when you are, in fact, asking people to pay for your services.

Choosing the right channels for you and your business will go a long way toward bringing this paradox into an aligned plan that has heart and gives you the results you seek. Have fun exploring my top six marketing channels in the following chapters.

You get to do what you most love to do, at the same time as letting the world know what you have to offer. It is different for everyone, and yet there are some ways that I have found that work best and are the most entertaining for others to learn from.

Make Marketing Fun for YOU

When I evolved my business to a sustainable success, I was asked by my minister to do an interview with her in front of the congregation one Sunday.

At that time, my niche was relationships, helping women in search of romantic love. My minister had been one of the people I had helped. Though we weren't going to focus just on romance, she believed I had wisdom to share.

Although this was something I was going to do for my church, I was also aware it was a wonderful marketing opportunity. Surely there would be a couple of single ladies in the congregation. Women with an entrepreneurial spirit who were looking for a soulmate.

So along with preparing for the interview, I brought along my Heart-to-Heart Connection Card Deck as giveaways for everyone in the church. I wrapped up a flyer with a little info on my business and tied each one with a pretty ribbon to the card deck.

I was surprised at how much I liked doing that interview. Speaking to a crowd about my stories and experience in the area of relationships was fun. I was also heartened by the response I received.

Many people who greeted me in the receiving line after the service told me how much they had learned from what I shared. I made a difference!

They were really grateful for my card deck as well, delighted to be given a pretty gift to take home. I enjoyed pointing out how the cards were both a way of connecting heart to heart, while at the same time being an actual card deck that they could use to play rummy.

I was hooked. I saw in that one experience that I could speak to audiences and have fun and impact. I got that having a product I could give people was a wonderful way to expose them to my work.

Just a few days later, I got a phone call from someone who heard my interview. She had never been to the church before, but something compelled her to go that morning.

She read the flyer attached to the card deck and was curious about what I offered. By the end of that chat, I had a new client!

Then, a few weeks later, I received an email from another woman who had attended church often and was surprised by my interview. She hadn't seen the connection between her spiritual path and her relationship issue before.

She wanted to know more and signed up for my blog.

Within a few months after receiving my weekly messages, she sent another message asking for a consultation. She soon became a client and member of my Women's Alchemy Coaching Circle for many years to come.

I was thrilled to have found a new way to market my business that was fun and effective. I wished that I had figured this out earlier! I could have saved myself a lot of drama and grown my business quicker.

And I was tickled at how it connected with another fun marketing strategy I had been using for years.

Because I love to write, I launched a newsletter in the startup stage of my business. I love to share stories about the human condition as I see it. This newsletter got a huge boost when I added 3000 names to my list.

You read that right! This was back in the days before inboxes were inundated with junk and before email marketing was regulated. I had just produced my relationship playing cards and discovered my big mistake with my engaged couples niche.

I was looking for another outlet to use the cards and promote my relationship coaching offers.

There was an organization called Smart Marriages that showed up on my radar. They held a big event once a year. This event brought together the general public, specifically people interested in taking relationship workshops, with top relationship experts of the time.

Some of my heroes, like Harville Hendrix, who created Imago Relationship Therapy, would be there. My interest was certainly piqued by this opportunity. I read through all the options available, and saw I was too late to sign up to host a workshop. They did, however, have a couple spaces available to rent a booth in the area where people sold books and other products related to relationships.

The price was steep. More than I had in my business budget at the time. It would require an expensive flight and hotel stay on top of the booth expense. I was ready to say no, not now, maybe next year, then something caught my eye.

One of the perks of having a booth was being given the contact information of everyone at the event. Along with all the information came permission to put all the names on my mailing list. Get out of town! I saw in a flash I could have 3000 plus email addresses of people in my niche, which I could then add to my newsletter list! Holy Cow!

By the end of the day, I had utilized my business line of credit and sealed the deal on the booth and all the rest.

This gave my business a big lift. Not all at once, but over time I heard from people responding to the stories and information in my newsletter.

It gave me the encouragement I needed to up the level of my newsletter to a blog that soon became one of my main marketing activities.

I learned from this experience that the most important thing I could do was to keep going. Though it was super fun to get 3000 names all at once, the truth is the business that came from this list came slowly.

I had a few inquiries and nice messages from my colleagues. Then some of them made their way to consultations and then became paying customers. Others made referrals, which are the mainstay of any coaching business. That was fifteen years ago and some of those people are still on my email list.

Inspirational Entertainment

I like to refer to the activity of getting your message out in a way that you like, and in which brings your message alive for others to enjoy, as Inspirational Entertainment, or IE. Through IE, you get to spread the good news about the possibilities of living a fulfilling life, honoring personal values, and having success through meaningful work.

I use this term because when we are entertained we can relax and take in otherwise obscure or far out concepts. It also allows us to understand a message on a deeper level that bypasses fear and confusion.

Plus, it's a great way to become known to your tribe, build a list, and gain followers. As I am sure you have noticed, inspirational entertainment correlates closely with marketing and is a necessary tool for successful marketing.

The key is to choose a couple of pathways and use them consistently without expecting overnight success, or even success in a few months, or success at all, for that matter!

I promise you, if you choose the form that brings forward your gifts, you will have fun *and* grow your business with joy. Are you ready? Let's go!

Next you get to choose the inspirational entertainment channels that are right for you in the evolution of your business as you use your talents.

Coaching may help people with serious stuff, but it is also a modality that lends itself to creative self-expression and fun I think it is hugely valuable to connect to your own experience while doing this, so you can connect with others in an authentic and compelling way.

There are myriad ways to broadcast your message—from delivering a short marketing message to offering a full-blown blast of credibility through channels like:

- Writing a blog
- Publishing a book
- Speaking

- Producing your own physical product
- Hosting a radio show or podcast
- Live streaming or YouTube videos

Each of these can be a channel for your creative expression, if it's right for you. That's the important factor to consider when choosing which type of IE you want for your business.

Here are some questions to consider:

- Does it fit with the style and purpose of your business?
- Does it fit your talents and strengths?
- Is your business in a stage that can use it optimally now? Or would it be better to wait?
- Does it bring you joy?

There are many different ways to go, so choose the one that works best for you at that time. Each type has similar qualities, activities, and purpose. Each one also has a whole host of differences.

One mistake I made (and I often see other coaches make) is to spend time and money pursuing a form of IE that doesn't match the criteria above.

Another mistake I ran into when developing my IE was having an expectation of the purpose that was incorrect.

Knowing the purpose and the results you intend to achieve up front will ensure that you put your time and effort to good use.

Through the iterations of soul-driven success that I have experienced, I have done just about everything in the book in this area.

For a long time, I puzzled over why some of it worked really well and other efforts fell flat in the marketplace.

Doing my own research and gathering the experience of other coaches, I have been able to see why some worked and how I got off track with others.

My intention is for you to learn not just about which form works best for you now, but to be able to continue making good choices as your business grows and new options appear in the marketplace.

So, pay attention to how you make your decisions, including all the factors named above.

When you do, you will naturally choose the best ways to use your IE as you work your way to new levels of success.

Through inspirational entertainment you get to spread the good news about the possibilities of living a fulfilling life, honoring personal values and having success through meaningful work.

What's important is learning to make your choices based on the stage your business is going through, your niche, your talents and the purpose you intend to use this channel to accomplish.

When all those come together with a big YES, it's magical. You will have fun and your business will prosper.

A Blog that Sizzles

Once I realized that writing was something I loved, and it could bring me business through a newsletter or blog, I decided to make it my main channel of marketing.

Over the evolution of my business, I shifted my niche a few times. Having written a newsletter based on relationships for many years, I found myself at one of those crossroads of evolution.

I was still doing a lot of relationship coaching work and was now including work with leaders and spiritual entrepreneurs. One afternoon while brainstorming with some fellow business owners, I had a flash of insight. I wanted to make my message lighter and shorter.

To not be tied down to my old niche, yet have time to explore the niche that was emerging. I decided I would start something fresh and call it The Kat Flash.

Something in this shift was a hit with my readers. They loved the new format, and new business came streaming in like never before.

I believe this happened for a few reasons. I was very intentional in what I wanted to write and whom I wanted to reach.

I made it more entertaining by keeping it short and light, even when the topic was deep. I was passionate about what I was doing in my work and that came through in the message each week. It gave me the opportunity to highlight any live events or new offerings in my business in a friendly way.

Writing a blog is an excellent way to give voice to what you care about, to connect with people in a deeper way, and to build your list.

The following exercises will help you break down the steps of creating and posting a blog.

The foundational activity of a blog or newsletter is developing, nurturing, and growing your list. Beyond that, to ensure your content sizzles, consider these:

Questions to explore:

- What are the problems you help people solve?
- What are the main interests of the people on your list?
- What is the core message of your business?
- What types of things do you like to write about?
- Some components you will need:
- A love of writing
- True stories that make the points you want to make
- Real life examples that can include facts, research, resources, and quotes
- Images to bring your blog to life

- A call to action so people will interact
- Important things to consider:
- Do you want to publish a newsletter or a blog or both?
- How often do you want to publish?
- Where do you want your blog to live?
- What platform/software will you use to send your blog or newsletter?
- How often do you want to promote an offering through your blog or newsletter?
- How do you want to use your blog on social media?
- How do you want to engage with people who respond?

Use the information you gathered from these questions to fill in the handy chart found on my website.

Extra Credit

Give yourself thirty minutes of uninterrupted time. Brainstorm fifty-two topics that are based on the problems people want you to help them with, your message, and your interests. That way you will have a topic for each week of the year. Use this list of topics as a jumping off place to write your blog or newsletter consistently and on purpose!

It's Showtime!

Radio shows, podcasts, YouTube channels, live streaming, and more!

When my husband, Curtis, and I first started our coaching business together, we chose The Relationship Coaching Company as our business name. We were looking for ways to engage with a new community that we had just moved to and ways to market our relationship coaching services.

At a business fair, we ran into a man who was in the AM radio business. His job was to sell ads and to enroll new hosts to begin shows in the time slots his station had available.

This sounded like a wonderful way to market our business. I had grown up with radio and there are many radio shows, especially the ones that are live or have a story-driven format, that I love to this day.

For many years, I listened to "The Diane Rehm Show" and imagined myself as host of my own show someday.

So, to have an opportunity like this, well, it felt like a dream come true.

We had to audition in order to be given a coveted Saturday morning time slot. The producer gave me the heads up to begin. I picked up that mic and started talking; it was like I had done it all my life. I was in!

Once we got the green light to do our show, we had to come up with a concept and marketing plan. AM radio is sponsor-based. In this case, the station would field our show to some current sponsors, and we would be on our own to find the rest.

I came up with a marketing format I thought would work well. It involved using my newsletter to find people interested in relationship tips. I would invite them to come on the show for some free coaching. Another aspect of the show would be to invite experts in the relationship field.

This is when I interviewed best-selling authors and relationship experts Gay and Kathlyn Hendricks!

Curtis co-hosted the show with me. He is a therapist as well as a relationship coach and his experience added to the show's credibility.

In the year we had our AM radio show, which we called "Partners in Paradise," we learned a ton about how to put on a show and how to successfully market it to our own folks. The issue we had with it was it was a lot of work, money, and effort to put on the show and do the marketing. We didn't have the time or inclination to find sponsors.

We were also not at a stage in our business that could fully handle this added amount of work. In hindsight, I would have worked to shore up our systems first. The other lesson learned from this experience was to decide ahead of time how I was going to get sponsors, or how to make the finances work without them.

I jumped in too soon. This show was wildly fun and did bring in new business, but it wasn't enough to warrant the output, so we closed it down after about a year.

In the years since, I have done a variety of online "radio" shows and even a Facebook live stream TV show! I am now starting a YouTube channel and finding much of my experience from the AM radio show has come in handy.

And, I have discovered, there are tons of YouTube experts who can help with the nuts and bolts if you choose to have your own show.

With each of them I have learned a lot about this type of entertainment, as it pertains to a coaching business. Since I love speaking and performing and it ties in with my writing, it has usually paid off.

The biggest lesson is one I speak of often in this book. Look at the stage of business you are in. Having a show can be a whole business in and of itself. Do your research and make clear choices on time, money, and the effort you can give to your show. Also, make sure you can connect the dots to the new business. When you do this, you will find having a show to be fun and fruitful.

OR

If you don't want to host your own show or podcast, you can always choose the option of being a guest on another person's platform or co-host with someone who is more experienced or who has a built-in audience.

It's essential to know how and where a show will fit into your marketing efforts.

Will you have a theme that connects to your business so you can speak about what you do? Will you invite guests to bring their wisdom AND their own followers? What type of show is most likely to be of interest to your people?

Here are some things you will want to consider if having a show appeals to you.

1. What results do you want to get from having a show or podcast?
2. Research the options available online and on AM or FM stations.
3. Consider the costs of putting on a show.
4. What equipment do you need?
5. What marketing will you need in order to have your people listening?
6. What ways can you be a guest on someone else's show?
7. What is the format that suits you best?
8. What would be the easiest way to get started?

I'll say it again, it's important to remember that the key to success is consistently delivering your message in an entertaining way.

This means that you will be creating and delivering material on a regular schedule. Only choose this option if you can and LOVE to do that. If you do, you will be richly rewarded.

Your Tangible Product

One of my first forays into having a physical product that aligned with my business happened quite by accident. My coach and I were brainstorming possibilities of ways to market my relationship coaching services to engaged couples. My coach said, "How about cards?" meaning congratulations-on-your-engagement kind of cards, but my brain popped to another type of card—playing cards!

So much is virtual these days that a tangible product seemed like it would be even more valuable in the marketplace. This idea for cards became one of my first tangible products. I named the card deck Staying Engaged. As you might recall, my niche at the time was engaged couples.

My vision was a deck of cards with questions on one side and the usual card stuff on the other. I love when creative ideas just float in like that!

I didn't know all that I know now, so I hadn't figured out the purpose of this product and how it aligned with growing my business.

I will admit, I had grand ideas! I saw my cards being sold at gift shops and bookstores around the world!

When I get an idea that comes through that channel, I jump on it. I immediately went to work thinking of what questions engaged couples most needed to ask each other.

I investigated companies that made custom card decks. I was amazed to find there are thousands of options out there to help you produce a tangible product.

It was surprisingly easy to come up with the questions. I knew what these couples were thinking about. Where they had issues that were hard to face and the dreams they harbored during this magical time in a relationship.

I came up with my top fifty-two questions, which I mixed up according to suits, and then I included jokers.

Some questions were serious, others were playful, and the jokers were downright wacky! I chose a card company based in India that was affordable and had an easy-to-use platform from which to produce the cards.

I hired my talented niece, Casey, who is a graphic artist, to design the artwork for the cards. It was an exciting time for sure! Coincidentally, by the time the cards were in production, Curtis had just proposed, and I had said YES!

We decided to throw a big party to celebrate the cards' birth into the world. The cards were due to land on the docks of Los Angeles about a week before February 14 so we made it a Valentine's Day party.

We invited all our family and friends and decided to announce our engagement during the party. Everything was in place. The food, the drinks, the help. We had done some marketing too, and invited people who we thought would help us promote the card decks.

Then the message came. The card decks were stuck on the tarmac in Singapore! It was the Chinese New Year and everything was shut down. The cards would not arrive in time. Thankfully, Curtis got on the phone and called the card company and any official he could think of to get those cards to us.

Miraculously, it worked.

The cards arrived the day before the party and the celebration was grand. After the party dust settled though, I realized that I hadn't fully thought out how we would use the playing cards.

Now, let's pause for the big lesson. Actually, two. Be aware of holidays that could derail your plans! And be intentional around the purpose and use of your tangible product before you have an inventory of 3,000 items in your living room.

We decided to price the cards low and went to business expos, networking events, and bridal shows hawking the cards. I found that having a beautiful stack of playing cards was attractive.

We made up challenges, giveaways, and contests for people to play at these events. One of the most rewarding experiences these cards brought was the conversations the questions triggered when people picked a random card. Conversations that led to an interest in our services!

The contacts we made at some of these events are still bringing in referrals a decade later. We grew our email list and established ourselves as relationship experts with the people we met through our tangible product.

After a lot of positive feedback from many people who used them in ways I never would have imagined, I found the cards' purpose. They became my "calling cards." A simple way to engage people around their relationship issues and dreams.

An Army of Interest

One of my favorite experiences with a tangible product happened at an event called Smart Marriages where Curtis and I had a booth and engaged in many meaningful conversations with people wanting relationship guidance. We also made some great contacts with other professionals.

The one that stands out to this day was with a man who oversaw marriage counseling for the army. The whole friggin' ARMY of the United States!

He thought since these were actual playing cards they might appeal to the men who would otherwise want to avoid the questions on the back side of each card.

After the event, we continued the conversation. At one point, it looked like our product was going big time with an order in the thousands! It all fell through due to bureaucratic red tape, but that potential "army of interest" gave me a glimpse of what's possible.

Do you have an idea for a tangible product that relates to your business? It could be quite simple, like our card deck, or a more complex game.

The pathway to producing a tangible product depends on the product itself. If you have a dream of creating a tangible product, I encourage you to think through the following questions before plunking down your hard-earned cash.

Here is a simple exercise to get you started:

1. What's the experience you want your product to give people?
2. What product would enhance the experience your clients have with you?
3. What product could you give away or sell at a price low enough to engage people in your services?
4. What's a product into which you'd be willing to invest your time and money so that it benefits your business?

Once you have determined what type of product you want to create and what it will do for your business, it's time to do some research.

- Conduct online searches to see what's out there.
- Post your ideas on social media and ask relevant experts.
- Go on an adventure to websites, as well as brick-and-mortar stores, to see if there are any clues, intuitive nudges, or outright examples of products you imagine would be perfect for you.

When you have enough information to move forward, it's time to look for producers of your type of product. Go through the same steps for this stage until you are ready to go into production!

I will leave you with this: Creating and producing a product is a great way to grow your business. A simple card deck, coloring book, or widget could be the calling card your business needs. So I say, Go for it!

Your Book is Born

Long before I even had an inkling I would start a coaching business or anything like it, I was aware that all my heroes wrote books. During the two decades prior to hanging out my coaching shingle, I was addicted to reading self-help books.

I especially loved the books with exercises. Soon I discovered that many of these authors also had workshops. I will never forget reading *Getting the Love You Want* by Harville Hendrix in the 90s. I fell in love with that book and did every single exercise.

I was trying to save my first marriage and I was willing to do whatever it took. On a Saturday evening, I was studying one of the exercises intently and the author mentioned one of his workshops that really helped couples in trouble. I looked to the back of the book to see if there was any information on these workshops, and sure enough, there was a website reference.

I hopped right on it and found that Harville himself was offering a workshop in New York City the very next weekend!

I moved heaven and earth to get there. It was a life changing experience. Not only did I learn a ton about relationships, but it piqued an interest to help others in this area.

The workshop was not enough to save my marriage, but it sparked something in me. I had been dipping my toes into the writing realm inspired by Julia Cameron's book *The Artist Way*. I had written a couple of plays and even an article for a self-help magazine.

I wondered if I too could write a book that would inspire people.

When I moved to Los Angeles in 2001, I joined the ICF chapter there and was an avid attendee. I loved hanging out with coaches and there were some fabulous speakers.

One speaker, in particular, became a mentor for me. Her name is Chellie Campbell and is the author of *The Wealthy Spirit*. I bought her book and loved it so much I signed up for her workshop, Financial Stress Reduction.

Here it was again. An inspiring author who had taught me a lot in her book and then offered to help me make that wisdom real with a workshop.

I wanted to do that too!

I had seen another inspiring author, Laura Berman Fortgang, who appeared at an ICF conference promoting her coaching book *Take Yourself to the Top*. She seemed to have the book-to-workshop thing down, so I hired her to help me take myself to the top with a book and workshop duo.

I wrote and self-published a book. By self-published, I don't mean the way you can self-publish these days. I literally paid a printer to print 100 slim copies of my book *It's Not Just a Wedding, It's Your Life*.

I will never forget the day the box of books arrived. I was so fricken' proud of myself! I created my own relationship workshop and now I had a book.

It was the kind of thrill that let me know this was not a one-time thing for me. I loved writing and having a book that was connected to my coaching program and workshop was truly fulfilling.

I wrote that book during the startup stage of my business evolution. I must admit I had high hopes for what it would do for my business. In retrospect, I can see this may not have been the ideal time to put my faith in a book.

I also see that it was a great thing to do. It did help my business and it was a beginning for me. I have no regrets.

I am very proud to have followed in the footsteps of so many of the people I most admire. The ones I have learned the most from.

I wrote my second book, *The Art and Science of Romance*, during the sustainable success stage of my business. I found it to be a wonderful doorway for the people I most wanted to work with to understand how I could help them.

My third book, *The Soulsearch*, was what I consider my first real published book. It contains the magic formula I discovered that leads to conscious creation. It has a lot of my life story and that of my business-building experience.

It was published as I was doing some soul searching of my own after years of sustainable success. I was yearning for my business to have more spiritual ground.

If you also love to write, publishing a book is both a thrilling emotional experience and can be one of the most important things to elevate your business in the marketplace.

I am not a writing coach. Although I love to write and know a lot about what works to be a compelling writer, that is not my area of expertise.

The focus here is for you to look at the purpose of writing and publishing a book first, before you make all the other choices that go along with this exciting but usually awfully long process.

Ask:

1. Do you want to write a book to satisfy your soul?
2. Do you want to write a book to grow your business?

3. Do you want to make money selling your book?

4. Would you like to do all three?

If you answered yes to the first question, I suggest you go forward and put your whole heart into your writing.

Your book may have nothing to do with your business, and that's fine. Set your expectations on writing something you are passionate about.

That alone is worth doing. You may find ways to tie it into your business promotion later. You may find that expressing your passion is exactly what you need to do to enjoy your business and connect with people your way.

If you said yes to the second question, I suggest you begin with an eBook that focuses on an offer you have in your business.

Writing this type of book can be fulfilling in that it will connect you to what you do in a new way, and it will give you a great tool to educate and enroll people in what you offer in your business.

If you answered yes to the third question, you will want to make sure that your soul's passion and your business are in alignment. Consider these questions:

- What book is your soul longing to write?
- What stories do you most want to tell?
- How do these stories connect with your business?
- What makes the most sense to include?
- What little darlings don't fit and would be better used in another way?

These are the questions will lead you to choices you will want to make first—before you dive into all the other questions about format, writing style, and how to publish.

Once you clearly know the purpose of your book, you can go full steam ahead.

Here are my suggestions for your first steps:

1. Dedicate time to writing every week.

2. Find an accountability partner or group.

3. Look honestly at what kind of help you will need, and get that help!

4. Research and choose a structure for your book.

5. Write, and then write some more, until it becomes a habit.

6. Put samples of what you are writing in articles, blogs, or social media posts to find out how it will land with people.

7. Give yourself time to play around with your writing AND take the discipline seriously.

8. Dump everything you want to write on the page and worry about editing later. Writing and editing employ very different parts of your brain and are best done separately!

9. Be willing to write many drafts!

10. Did I say to write...and keep writing? Yes! Your love of writing will guarantee that you finish your book.

Once you have a first draft, and are clear on how you want to use the book, it's time to research how to publish it.

My last words of wisdom here are, you can't go wrong. Writing a book is always a good thing.

If you are so inspired, begin writing today!

Public Speaking

You may remember me mentioning my entrepreneurial spirit at a young age. I told you about how I earned money by putting on plays and charging admission to the play.

This passion of mine was up leveled when my 5th grade teacher was so impressed with my play about Sacagawea that she arranged for me to perform it in every single class at our middle school. What a treat that was! I got out of class and had a blast performing the words I had so lovingly written.

As you read in Part 3, when I was 12, I was asked to write and give the confirmation speech for my large Methodist church congregation. There were about a thousand people who attended live and it was also broadcast on the radio.

At the time my mother was in the hospital dying of cancer. I knew how much my confirmation meant to her, as she asked me about it often.

She was going to be able to hear me on that early spring Sunday from her hospital bed. I was not one bit nervous as I stepped up to the pulpit to speak.

I had written my script very carefully to be one that made my mom proud. It contained a little bit of the truth, but in all honesty it was mainly a shined up version of that truth, meant to impress my Sunday school teachers and assure my mom that I was on the right spiritual path.

I delivered the speech well. No stammering or stumbling over my words. I felt at home speaking into that mic.

My mom passed away that night. I never got to speak to her after my speech to see if it had the impact I intended. I knew I had sold out on my own truth and as I grieved my mother's death

I wondered if it had been worth it. I believe during that grieving time my speaking up and selling out got all tangled up.

This traumatic experience probably contributed to my becoming absolutely terrified of ever speaking in public again. Something in me turned off during that time.

I think there are many experiences that lead to many people being unnecessarily afraid of public speaking.

For me though, I knew it was something I loved. Public speaking was in my blood, and I had experienced the pure joy of having my words received by an audience. I knew the impact that was possible, and I longed to experience it again.

The pivot came when I was attending a year-long course based on the five elements of Chinese Acupuncture at SOPHIA, School of Philosophy and Healing in Action. One cold winter Saturday, the leader noticed my silence in the group, and asked me about it. She asked if I would be willing to do some work in front of the class. Sure, why not? I was merely TERRIFIED of public speaking.

Instead of speaking, she asked me to sing one of my favorite songs. Hallelujah. I started to sing. Then there was a circle of people singing with me, louder and louder they sang, and I found my voice again in that hallelujah chorus!

It didn't happen overnight, but slowly I started experimenting with speaking up. This was when I gave a talk to my church about my experience of selling out with my confirmation speech.

I had learned about the manifesting practice I shared with you of Acting As If. I tried it with public speaking during a training I was a part of in my role with the Postal Service. I still felt the fear but also the joy of having an impact on my fellow trainees.

A few months after that experience, I received a phone call out of the blue with an invitation to become a trainer for the postal service. To lead trainings at all the post offices in my area. I love how the Universe works! I had stepped out of my comfort zone to grow myself in an area that mattered to me. And the Universe responded with the ideal opportunity to do public speaking to small groups. Lots and lots of speaking, which turned into a job that lasted for the remainder of my career with that organization.

I write this story for those of you who also long to have an impact with your words, yet are afraid to get out of your comfort zone. You may be terrified, like I was, or simply blocked by fear of failure.

Here is the rest of the story that I hope will bust any fears you might have and encourage you to Speak Up!

I kept working on this fear for years. I went through a leadership program that required me to get up in front of the room AND to make videos of my leaders skills. I took a class called Speaking of Stories, which culminated in a live performance in a theatre.

I signed up for a Ted Talk boot camp where I had to write and perform a speech that would be critiqued by my teacher and peers. I didn't just deliver the talk once, but three times!

Then the Universe gave me another opportunity. My minister asked me to deliver a sermon while she was on vacation. It was the perfect opportunity to finally let go of my fear for good. I took that boot camp speech and honed it into a sermon. I didn't miss the irony that the last time I stood before an audience without fear was also in front of a church!

I practiced and prepared and memorized that sermon. The story I told was one of my most vulnerable. The story of my kidnapping.

I knew on the morning I was to deliver the sermon that I had done it. No more fear.

I walked up to that pulpit with confidence. I stood grounded in myself as the sermon flowed through me. And I beamed with joy when I received a standing ovation. My minister said, "Masterful. That was masterful, Kat."

I had done it. Conquered my fear and had the exact impact I wanted to have on the congregation. I had been vulnerable and willing to be uncomfortable. I also was standing for what I believed and letting people know about my book and my business.

Don't let fear stand in the way of using your voice to impact others and grow your business.

Speak Up!

I have heard it said that there are three basic ways to promote a coaching business. Writing. Networking. Speaking.

I have found this to be true, no matter how much the times have changed.

Speaking is a sure-fire way to let people know what you do and, at the same time, have a positive impact. There are so many ways to use speaking as an asset in your business.

Some coaches find they like speaking so much, they make a career out of it. There is a whole track you can follow to become a sought-after and well-paid speaker.

This worksheet is focused on the kind of speaking you can do where money is not your main aim.

Some of these types of speaking options are:

- Networking events
- Business events
- Business organizational meetings
- Transformational trainings
- Online summits
- Niche-focused groups

Getting booked into these places is usually simple. The work is in choosing the places where there will be people interested in topics you want to talk about.

Here is a game plan you can use to get out in the world and speak up!

Make a list of topics you would like to talk about that relate to your business. Start here:

- Stories and examples you can use to deliver your message
- The benefits and results you can promise the audience
- Problems your topic addresses
- Dreams you help people make real
- What you are most passionate about
- Areas of life in which you want to become an authority

One way to play around with these idea starters is to write your answers on index cards. Then match them up in a variety of ways to see what combinations excite you the most.

Then, choose one to three topics and reach out to people you know and to networking and business groups to get a sense of where your speaking offer is most welcome.

Book your first speaking gig!

Next, write your signature speech. By using all the information you have gathered, and what you learned from the chapter A Message that Matters, this part will be pretty easy!

You can find templates online that will help you structure your speech or ask your coach for resources.

The final steps are:
- Prepare for your talk.
- Practice giving the speech a few times so you can hear how it sounds. The spoken word lands much differently than the written.

- Get feedback from peers or join a Toastmasters International club and deliver the speech a few times.
- Modify it based on the feedback you receive.

Include in the speech a call to action:

- How people can contact you
- Sign-up sheets for your email list
- Offer discounts just for the audience if they act today
- Give them a next step they can take to further their learning on your topic

Organizations, clubs, and businesses are always looking for speakers with an inspiring message. People respond well to someone who stands in front of a room and teaches a relevant topic that inspires new ideas.

Depending on the stage of your coaching business, you might want to find paid speaking gigs.

Look for places where you will be speaking to your ideal customers and speak of topics that connect directly to your business offerings.

And don't forget that nowadays, speaking up is easier than ever before. You can simply push record on your camera phone and post a message on social media to have an impact. We are all hungry to hear authentic stories that show us the way forward.

Online Engagement

There are many options for you to utilize social media to be seen and known as a coach. There are so many ways you can engage on Facebook, LinkedIn, Instagram, and other social media outlets.

You can post your blog or podcast or go live with a video that engages your ideal client. You might offer a question about your program topic and start an online conversation.

The most important thing to remember is to keep it simple and be consistent with your postings so you can generate an interest in what you have to offer. Always give value with your posts beyond talking about what you offer.

Post challenges, share exercises, or put out a question that starts a conversation in which you comment. Remember to keep it entertaining. Even if it is a serious topic you are addressing, you want to engage people, not hit them over the head with your ideas.

Ask friends to share your posts and your blog messages. Share in communities you belong to and that are aligned with your beliefs.

Use the platform you are most familiar with, and you will connect with people who already know and trust you.

The purpose is to create and continually engage with a group of people in your niche who love your message.

I interviewed Global Community Builder and Social Media Marketing expert, Lynn Abaté-Johnson. I wanted to find out what is most important for coaches to consider regarding online engagement when promoting their business.

Here is what she had to say:

First, look at what has always worked. Before social media and digital marketing, what worked was looking people in the eye and building relationships over time. Social media simply allows you to build those relationships more globally and at scale.

Social media is best used to create awareness, a community, and to help build your email list. The most important use of social media is to drive traffic to your website. Creating a strong presence on the right social media channels makes it easy for people to find you and do business with you.

With help, do the work to figure out your identity as a coach. Put the foundational pieces of your niche, message, and brand in place. Then get help with your marketing. Hire people to do things that are not in your wheelhouse, like someone who knows about community building who can help translate your vision into content that compels people to reach out to you.

Choose one channel to "master." See what works there, and then add another platform, layer –by –layer, as you grow your business. Implement, experiment, and see what works for at least six months. Adjust your expectations and be patient.

Once you have established an online presence, it has to be consistent and aligned with your message. Digital marketing, including social media marketing, is a long game of relationship building, based on people getting to know, like, and trust you.

Another way of spreading your message is through word of mouth. When you are posting on social media, the last thing people want to see is, "I am so great. You should hire me to be your coach."

What people like, and what they are responding to, is that you are a real human being. The medium doesn't matter; it is how you stand with your stake in the ground. There is plenty of business for everybody, which is what coaches and entrepreneurs who carry an abundance mindset experience.

They have this Soul Driven purpose which is solid. The key is under-standing your value. It is managing your own expectations. Most businesses, no matter what they are, take three years to really be profitable.

Freebies—It's Like Ice Cream

Many years ago, I attended a coaching conference and came across a booth that was using a very clever concept. They were handing out tasting spoons, just like you would find at an ice cream parlor, with their business info on them.

The booth was hosted by a marketing company, and their message was that, as a coach, you needed to give potential customers a *taste* of what you offer.

Just like when tasting ice cream, it is much easier to make a choice and plunk down the money when you already know a little bit about what you are eating, or in this case, buying.

Coaching is a personal business that can be hard to describe in words. If that's the case, what do you think will move people to work with you?

I agree that an excellent incentive is to give them a taste of the results they can expect when they engage your services.

These are sometimes called lead magnets, but I prefer the term freebies.

Learn to create the exact freebies that will give your ideal client an experience of what you offer in a way that compels them to want more.

The best freebies solve a problem! Here are some ideas to get you started:

- A simple one-page report or article that identifies and helps your ideal client solve a problem.

- An assessment that gives your ideal client insight on their strengths or weaknesses.

- An e-book that addresses a common issue your niche struggles with.

- A quiz that gives your ideal client a whole new way of thinking about their life.

- An entertaining experience, such as a video that invites further engagement.

- A short training that is a part of your coaching offer.

- An exercise you have made into a PDF with your logo and contact info.

- A webinar or Zoom call where you do part of your coaching program or an exercise that immediately impacts your potential clients.

Or, a freebie could be as simple as a 30-minute session or consultation.

In every stage of a coaching business, it is important to have ways people can experience a taste of what you do for free.

Your free offer needs to solve a problem, but it should NOT be giving away the store. This is not about being stingy; it is about integrity.

Like the ice cream sample, it works best when you give just the right amount. Then people are compelled to find out more about what you do, or help them realize they are not interested, which saves you both a lot of time and energy.

Weave the creation and offering of freebies into your ongoing marketing system. Keep testing to discover what engages your ideal clients. Don't get too attached to any of them...keep creating different ones and seeing how they work.

Nuggets

- The different types of IE work together beautifully. A blog promoting a speech, a talk tying into a book, a book with your business offering at its heart. A show that connects with your tangible product.

- There are so many ways to mix and match these tried-and-true forms of marketing. Use them to promote your business using your unconventional wisdom and creativity to get your message out in the world. Choose the ones you really love, and it will be fun for you and that joy will be infused in everything you do.

- Each type of IE requires work, don't get me wrong. Therefore, making choices that work best with your stage of business is the most likely way to bring you business. Then you can have the impact you most want through marketing activities that are sustainable.

- Regularly ask yourself what kind of marketing would you like to do. I have found that focusing on two at any given time, or possibly three at the most, works best.

1. Referrals
2. Networking
3. Social media
4. Blogs
5. Videos
6. Writing articles
7. Podcasts
8. Webinars
9. Free workshops

10. Speaking and presentations
11. A group such as a book club, Meetup, or networking group
12. Other (Use your imagination!)

I hope you have found this section as fun to read as it was for me to write! Come back and revisit this section often for inspiration about ways (both effective and fun) to attract a crowd.

For a coaching business, this means you will have a way to reaching people beyond those you already know. It is also a way for those you know to easily refer you to others. Referring someone to a blog, podcast or product is a great introduction to your work. Play around with the ways I have presented and other ways you have found that work for you. Ways that bring out your creative self-expression and allow your light to shine for others to see.

Part 5:

BUSINESS ESSENTIALS

There are no secrets to success. It is a result of preparation, hard work, and learning from failure.
—Colin Powell

Making money is art and working is art and good business is the best art.
—Andy Warhol

Systems and Structures Work!

One of the most important things you can do to create a stable foundation for your business is to set up systems, choose a structure, and get the help you need.

When I first started my career as a coach, I put some structures and systems in place. I knew myself well enough to know that I couldn't move forward without them.

There were the basics, like a good computer and phone system. Then I set up an office in my home. I believed in my business enough to spend the money and insist on having the space in my home. A business needs a place to be nourished and for you as coach to be able to work.

Next, I decided that my business structure would include group programs.

I started small with a weekly book club, and over time I played with different types of groups and programs. What worked for me as I described previously, and can work for you, was to reserve time in my calendar for the book club and eventually for my groups before they were "real" in the world. Remember the lesson of "acting as if." This is where you put it to action.

Create the structure first so you can invite people into a space— physical or virtual—that already feels secure, for both you and your clients.

Although at the beginning I wasn't making a lot of income, I knew that to generate a steady income I would need to have help with some of the details.

I hired a teenager who was really efficient and eager to learn about business. This was before there was such a thing as a virtual assistant! She helped me keep my schedule in order and work through my marketing strategies.

I also bartered with a bookkeeper who helped me set up all the financial aspects of my business in exchange for coaching.

There are so many more options today than there were in 2001. Now there are virtual assistants who are very experienced working with life coaches. How amazing is that? There are systems and processes geared specifically to support coaches and other solo entrepreneurs.

As different as the times are now, some things remain constant. To build a strong business, you need systems and support to help with marketing, scheduling, and the financial well-being of your business.

One of the reasons that you have this book in your hands right now is because I have an extraordinarily strong viewpoint, based on lots of experience, about the importance of having good systems, choosing the right structure, organizing business offerings and, of course, being clear on how the money works. It is a big part of my vision to pass this learning to you.

Let's Talk About Money

Money is at the center of any business and a coaching business is no different.

This involves a lot of exploration because you will need to assess growth of your business, how big or small you want it to become, and how much you are willing to invest in its growth.

You also will need to look at where you need the most support right now. Look at what covers the nuts and bolts of running a business, the things which may not have been top of your mind when you decided to make coaching your profession.

Most likely you were imagining the joy of helping people transform their lives! The systems and structures are what will help you do just that.

Exercise: Simple Systems

Take a minute to assess where you are right now in your coaching business.

In regards to systems, structure and support:

- What systems do you need to run your business? (e.g., website, email marketing system, accounting software, appointment scheduler)

- What is the structure of your business?

- What support do you need to integrate a soul-driven business into your life?

- How much do you want to charge?

- What type of packages or group offerings might you create?

- What are you willing to do to let people know about your offers?

When it comes to the money:

- How much do you need to spend to run your business?

- How many clients do you need to make a good living?

- What are the activities you need to do to sustainably and regularly enroll that many clients?

Before you fall over from exhaustion due to reading these lists, ask yourself:

- What support do I need right now?

- What help would make setting up my systems a whole lot easier and buckets more fun?

Now, imagine where your business will be in six months and where it will be in a year.

From those perspectives, consider the same questions above. You can see what systems and help you need to have in place to market, sell, schedule, and manage the money for your coaching business.

This simple exercise is critical to do again and again. I can't stress enough the importance of knowing that each choice you make will evolve through many evolutions and iterations of your business! At the end of this section is another exercise called *Add it all Up* that will help you keep your finances in order.

What Is a Business Model?

Internet search definition
A business model is the system in which ideas, people, and products come together to generate revenue.

The term "business model" actually can be traced back to the earliest days of business; it simply refers to how a business makes money.

For instance, a retail clothing store makes money by selling clothes to customers who need clothes. How it sells those clothes identifies the model it uses: a store at a mall, through an online website, a small store downtown, a pop-up store, or at a flea market. Or maybe a combination of these.

Similarly, a coaching business makes money by selling coaching services to people who want to make a change or achieve a goal. The model you choose determines HOW you will make the money.

Your business includes You, Your Message, Your Brand, and Your Niche...all brought together in a business model that brings you joy and profit.

You might choose to include in your business model individual coaching, group coaching, time-limited courses, products, and other services. It may also include working for an organization, in a partnership, or hiring other coaches to work for you!

Remember, you can always iterate from where you are now, but you need to make a choice to get your business into the marketplace. That's where you will find out what you really like and what is most profitable for your type of coaching. Hanging out on the sidelines creating the perfect business model is not going to produce better results. Use the information and internal guidance to choose a model, then get out and let the world and your intuition give you the feedback you need to make adjustments.

I have included examples of business models for coaches in this chapter. But first, I have a story that contains a lot of wisdom about a business model and more learning from my experience in the fruit business.

A Business Model for Fruit Growers

One of my lessons from being in the fruit growing business was how important having a business model is. Especially if want to make your business unique yet sustainable.

There is a common business model in the fruit growing industry that had been effective for many years. This model consists of owning a large amount of fruit orchards, growing apples, pears, peaches, and a variety of cherries and berries.

A small portion of this fruit wis sold at a fruit stand owned by the grower. A large portion is sold to a local processing plant.

This model is dependent on a few factors for the grower to make a good living. The grower needs to own a lot of land because the profit margin for fruit is small.

The benefit of this model for the growers is this gave them a guaranteed place to market their fruit without much effort. The downside is the grower has a lot of competition with the little fruit stand and is at the mercy of the processors who set the price for the bulk of their crop.

My first husband, Eddie, and his partners didn't like this model, so they looked at other business models for fruit growers. They discovered the farmer's market business model. This model was for growers with small amounts of land, selling fresh fruit directly to the public, which meant small labor costs and no middle man taking a cut of the profits. This appealed to them. So, they looked closer.

There were a lot of rules at these markets and a lot of competition. They decided to go with this model AND add in their own farmer's markets in church parking lots, where they had more control.

This model meant they didn't have to buy more land or have very many employees.

They also had the opportunity to grow exceptional fruit that would be valued and would garner a premium price in their niche market, which was mainly educated, well-off city dwellers.

Best Models for Coaches

A business model for a coaching business works much the same way. There are a few tried-and-true models out there that might appeal to you. Or you might be attracted to one that is a little more complex, or you might want to take a model you like and add your own unique twist.

I am going to lay out just a few business models that coaches use and encourage you to do a little research on your own.

Like everything else in this book, the goal is for you to pick one **for now** knowing you can iterate to another one at any time.

The most important thing to pay attention to (this is the "why you should care part," so pay attention!) is to choose a business model that makes sense at the intersection of your **effort, strengths, and profitability.**

Your business model isn't your product or service; it's not your price, niche, or offer. It's all of it working together to create an experience for yourself and your clients.

As a soul-driven success business owner, these elements need to work together in a way YOU like and feel good about.

There are a lot of different business models for coaches—from the simple ones shown below to more complex ones like evolving your business by hiring coaches to work for you, working with other coaches in partnerships, or creating your own certification programs.

The sky's the limit here. It is important, as you consider what business model works best for you, to remember the basic reason for choosing a model at all. It is YOUR system that brings together ideas, people and products so that YOU can generate revenue. Your business needs revenue to be healthy, strong and stable. In this vibrant state, it supports you so that you can help people the way only you can help them.

Below are a few coaching models to get you started. They top of the charts in popularity.

Coaching Model 1: Private Coaching

This is usually where most people begin their coaching practice.

Private coaching can be extremely lucrative because your brain and your time are the most expensive things you have.

As such, private coaching is typically seen as the high-end service a coach offers.

Additionally, it's typically (though not always) easier to sell one, high-priced product to one person than to sell a lower-priced product to many people. However, there are some cons to private coaching.

The main con is that it isn't scalable. Since you're operating in a one-to-one model, your income is limited by your time and energy.

Coaching Model 2: Group Coaching

As you see in my own examples throughout this book, one way to grow a coaching business is to move from private coaching to group coaching.

Group coaching is more scalable because it's a one-to-many coaching model, meaning you are helping multiple people at once.

If done correctly, and if it's something you like doing, this can help you make more money without burning out as some coaches do with private coaching.

A few examples of group coaching:

- Long-term group coaching: A six-month program or ongoing mastermind groups.

- Intensive group coaching: A one – or two-day workshop where several people participate.

- Short online workshop: Wide range of options on delivery models. For example, a one-time, 90-minute class or a four-week group coaching course.

There are many ways to enhance this type of business model, such as offering your clients opportunities for private coaching or other added-value services.

Coaching Model 3: Executive Coaching

With this model, you can choose to be in business for yourself and have contracts with organizations, work for a coaching company that contracts with organizations to provide executive coaching, or you can be an internal coach and earn a salary for coaching employees.

I work with many coaches who are interested in learning more about executive coaching. There are many similarities in the coach training phase and much of the foundational work in the startup phase as well.

Beyond that executive coaching has its own track. Since this is not my area of expertise, I interviewed a wonderful coach named Ann Farrell, CPCC, PCC, MGSCC. She is the founder and CEO of Quantum Endeavors and the Inpowered Coaching Institute and is renowned in this area. She helped me to glean a little insight for you.

When I asked her to give me the big picture, she reported this:

There is an openness in organizations not just for one-on-one coaching, but also the recognition and new levels of awareness of the need for more Humanness or whole-person focus in the organization. Front and center is the fact that the emotional and mental health of their employees is key to their level of engagement and, therefore, their results. Organizations recognize the value of investing in coaching for that purpose and more.

Ann's top three tips:

1. *If a coach has chosen the executive path, they need to be clear about their expertise. Organizations value experience and context as they need to know the coach understands what it takes to be successful, not just in general, but in their environment. The coach also needs to have an understanding of the general needs of organizations and do their own research before approaching organizations, instead of asking them "what keeps you up at night?"*

   What current "urgent and emergent" need does your expertise best enable you to credibly support and address?

2. *The best strategy is to land this work is to establish themselves as strategic partner, not a vendor. Organizations do not want more vendors. What they do want are people who can help them with their needs. When viewed as someone who can help, coaching is seen as a solution. Keeping your focus on the results the organization is looking for and how you can support them to achieve them is key. The organization is not necessarily attached to the "how" of coaching. What they are attached to is the outcome they seek. As a partner in solution, they need to trust you will help them address their needs.*

3. *How you structure your service offerings is very key. Specifically designing your coaching engagements to best address specific needs versus "one size fits all" enables you to create stronger results.*

Also key is having options that enable you to meet all their needs— including budget—while also honoring your value. Constructing your coaching offering so the outcomes and the process you use to meet all of their expectations is clear and easily understood gives confidence in your ability to provide them the support they seek while meeting all their expectations.

When approaching an organization, Ann advises coaches to expect the following:

Expect them to either directly ask or expect you to tell them "Why you?" as the coach they should entrust with our talent.

Supporting organizations to understand your experience and expertise is key as organizations have been investing in executive coaches for a very long time. Traditionally, executive coaches have been predominantly ex-CEOs or successful experts in their fields. They were viewed much like the star player-to-coach model in sports. Our profession has matured through the evolution of training in our industry and while organizations still value expertise and experience, they now also recognize and value formal coach training. More and more organizations are looking for coaches with ICF credentials.

The future for executive coaching is exciting. Industry data states that organizations today invest $365 billion annually in developing their talent and some project that to grow by 30-40 % over the next five years.

Coaching is becoming recognized more and more as the talent development investment with the greatest ROI. Current trends are the growth in leadership coaching specifically focused on elevating the

*leadership effectiveness of executives and leaders at all levels as just
one of areas projected to grow.*

There are many more business models that work for coaches! These
are just the three most common. Remember that there are myriad
ways you can take these popular models and mix and match to
make a model that really suits you and where you are with your
coaching career.

After reading about the top business models and doing your
own research, begin sketching out your business model using the
exercise below.

Exercise: Put It All Together and Go

To explore and choose the business model option that is right
for you, take some time to answer the following questions.

- Do you want to primarily do individual coaching?
- Would you like to have a program?
- Would you like to do group coaching?
- Would you like to have a workshop?
- Would you like to offer products?
- Would you like to work for an organization?
- Would you like to work in partnership with
  another coach?
- Would you like to have an outside gig?
- Would you like a combination of the above? If so, which
  combination?

Now, it's time to consider the financial aspect of your
business as well. I find it best to answer the questions in the
following exercise by looking ahead at the next six months

or a year. You can also do a version looking out five years to see how you would like your income to grow.

Exercise: Add It Up

How much money would you like to make from all elements of your coaching business in the 12 months?

Income over the course of the next 12 months:

- Total Monthly Amount
  - Session Income
  - Coaching Packages Income
  - Other Income

Now look out five years and answer the same questions:

- Total Monthly Amount
  - Session Income
  - Coaching Packages Income
  - Other Income

My income now:

My income in one year:

My income in five years:

This is a great exercise to do on a regular basis. Just play with it and see what feels good for now. Remember you are evolving your business and there will be many iterations.

Nuggets

- You need to set up systems and structure right from the start.

- The most important areas to consider are scheduling, the financial aspects, and marketing.

- Investing in your business will pay off.

- A business model is simply how your business makes money.

- Explore the models that are already working for coaches.

- Do your own research and introspection to find the model that suits you best.

Let's be honest. This section of the book might seem a little less inspiring than others. What I have found, though, is when you actually sit down and write out the numbers, chose a specific coaching model or create systems to make your work easier this creates a different kind of inspiration. You will feel more aligned with making your dream a reality instead of just wishing it would happen. That is a great feeling indeed!

Part 6:

GROUP COACHING AND ONLINE PROGRAMS

A leader takes people where they want to go. A great leader takes people where they don't necessarily want to go but ought to be.
—Rosalynn Carter

At this point, you have a lot of tools and ideas to help your coaching business grow and prosper. You've learned the importance of finding your niche, staying true to your vision, growing your business from the foundation up, marketing skills, and so much more. Adding in a group program or an online offering is the one thing you can do to leverage all of that knowledge. People love a program, and offering something online will make it much more accessible to those you most want to reach.

A Great Way to Grow

When I was in that transition stage of finishing my training and claiming coaching as my new career, I began experimenting with creative ways to market my business. In a brainstorming session with my coach, we hit on one thing I could do that rang all the bells for me: a book club.

I was a self-help book junkie so I saw this as an opportunity to come out of the closet with my obsession in a way that would be fun for me and hopefully others.

As luck would have it, I was also acquainted with the owner of a very cool bookstore in my small town of Gettysburg. When I approached her with my idea, she jumped on board. She offered to highlight my book selection as the shop's book of the month and to even include my contact information for anyone interested in joining the book club!

I chose the book *Taming Your Gremlin* as my first offering. I loved that book and used it often with my coaching clients to help them understand the concept of the saboteurs. Besides, it was super funny to boot.

On the night of the first meeting, I was excited and nervous. I had prepared everyone to read at least the first chapter of the book before their arrival. I had prepared a light snack for the group and a timeline to anchor the discussion, as well as a little exercise. I had NOT prepared myself for all the resistance that showed up in that first book club meeting.

Some of the participants didn't understand the gremlin concept, others just didn't like the book. Yikes! Luckily, there were a few who loved the book and wanted to dive into it. I learned from that experience that I could lead a book club, and maybe other groups, using my coaching skills—even when things got messy.

I worked with the resistance just like I would an individual client. It was magical to feel the shift happening, not only in those individuals, but in the whole group. I used the wisdom of those who were enthusiastic to bring new learning to the others. I was the leader, but I was leader/coach, which meant it was not all about ME or my opinion. The transformation came from the group and the individuals' combined growth.

I want to be truthful here. It was my first time with this kind of coaching. I had not been expecting the event to go this way, so there were moments when I was freaking out (inside)! I was in my own stuff, worried about what people would think. There were friends of mine, the bookstore owner herself, and others who I didn't know at all in attendance.

I was hooked, though. The atmosphere was so alive and electric! Something new had been created. Change was happening around us. It was palpable. I had experienced the power of group coaching and there was no going back.

Even to this day, having led thousands of group coaching sessions, I still find myself experimenting with what works for a specific group of people. There are so many variables! This makes group coaching exciting and will definitely keep you on your creative toes, sharpening your coaching and improvisation skills!

Ready...Fire...Aim

With all my experimenting, one thing that has always worked for me when it comes to creating my best group coaching experiences is to GO...to fire before I aim...which was when I would have everything all figured out.

You don't need to have it all figured out, but you DO need to have structure and a way of marketing.

As a coach, you will be able to bring value to your groups. The structure is very important, and the marketing is necessary if you want group coaching to be a sustainable element in your business.

I will never forget the year I did my New Year's visioning for my business and saw group coaching right in the center. Inspiring, yes. I loved group coaching, but I hadn't done it in a while. I had been focused on writing a book, having my radio show, and growing my individual coaching business. But there it was on the vision board, so I began dreaming about what kind of a group I wanted this time.

I got a hit that it would be a women's group. I saw a lot of women in a circle when I allowed myself to access my soul's wisdom. But I had nothing...nada...when it came to marketing ideas or the structure of this coaching group.

I touched on this story earlier in the book, but want to expand upon it here so you can benefit from my full experience.

It was early March when my minister called and asked to see me. I was honored and a bit surprised. We had talked often but she had never asked to see me on a professional level.

She came to my office with a story that was heavy on her heart. Her marriage was ending. She felt lost and alone. She knew I helped women with relationship issues so she asked me flat out. "Kat, would you be willing to start a women's group? Maybe some kind of women's circle."

My heart jumped for joy. I said YES and went to work. I know a good opportunity when I see one. I was prepared enough to just go for this one. I had one enthusiastic member and she knew a few women she would invite. I didn't really know what this coaching circle would look like, but I began talking about it with everyone

I knew. At my networking meeting, with current clients, with friends, and in my newsletter.

I imagined it would be an in-person event, as well as have a virtual component so I could offer it to clients of mine in different parts of the world.

I went pretty big right out of the gate. I set the time of the first in-person meeting. Then I offered three different call-in times for the virtual sessions.

What was I thinking?! That was perhaps a bit of putting the horse before the cart.

The first in-person meeting was amazing! Six wonderful women showed up and they were all in. There was a variety of ages and circumstances. Unhappily married, divorced, single for a while.

I had created a good structure to help the women feel safe and able to share their stories, while keeping it moving along with my coaching and a fun exercise. It was a success!

The virtual groups took a little more time to nurture. This was back in the day when it was unusual to gather online. On the first call, there was only one woman who showed up!

With three groups to get going at once, it took a while, and the learning curve was steep for me. I also had to keep the marketing moving forward as I was creating better and better structure.

About a year in, I had three dynamic virtual groups and a once a month in-person group that had grown into a cohesive group that welcomed the new members with love and grace.

My beloved Women's Alchemy Coaching Circles! As I shared earlier in the book, this group coaching program lasted over a dozen years and became the mainstay of my business until I evolved my business to a new niche.

Curriculum-based vs Process-based Groups

During the first year of growing my coaching circles, I realized there were two major types of group coaching programs: curriculum-based and process-based.

Once I saw this, it was a lot easier to move forward using these two types in different ways.

When I started my Women's Alchemy Coaching Circle, which I think of as a Feminine Mastermind Group, I began it as a process-based group. This had a structure which helped the women share and learn from each other. A process-based group does not have a curriculum and relies on a structure that allows for sharing and processing emotions and thoughts of the participants.

Then I started a program I called The Art and Science of Romance. I taught it as a six-week class. This was curriculum-based and followed a very clear timeline.

I offered The Art and Science of Romance virtually, three times over the course of a year. Many women in the class wanted continued support so they joined my coaching circle.

Some of the women wanted private coaching to support them in furthering the learning and growing they had done during the class. So, I added a private coaching offer specifically for that purpose.

That was when I started the Women's Alchemy Circle as a package, which included the ongoing process-focused group with private coaching options, all for a monthly fee.

Over the years, I have played around with offering these two types of groups along with private coaching. It evolved many times and is at the heart of my success as a coach.

Here's an important point to remember: The class, the ongoing circle, and my private sessions all focused on helping my niche reach their specific goals, overcome obstacles, and create fulfill-ment in the area they wanted it most.

That made it easy to deliver the results that my tribe most wanted to achieve.

I'm here to tell you that there are a million great ideas for classes, programs, offerings, events (on and on) that will pop into your mind. After all, you are infinitely creative! But remember the lessons of Chasing Shiny Object Syndrome? Keep focused and never lose touch with what your NICHE wants.

Your Program Starts Here

One of the biggest mistakes I have made in launching my many group coaching programs was starting with the curriculum rather than the people. The marketing was so much harder and leading the group wasn't as dynamic as the groups I lead where I started with a clear niche that I already knew wanted what I was offering.

And then I learned to start with the people.

Recall my first niche of women entrepreneurs who had a small business and who felt overwhelmed and discouraged in their work? They needed support and accountability. They loved their work but found it difficult to stay organized and have both business success and a full personal life.

Over the years, this evolved to successful women entrepre-neurs seeking a soulmate. These women were spiritual and the type of businesses they had meant they were leaders in their own communities.

The marketing—including group offerings—for this specific niche was fun and easy because I knew what they were afraid of, the pain they felt, and the dreams they held in their hearts. I knew I could help them! **So, I focused on the marketing first and created the content and structure to match the women who signed up. This is where the magic happens.**

Here are two examples:

My "Marketing First" experience:

As I related earlier in this chapter, I started a process-focused group called the Women's Alchemy Coaching Circle. This came about when a woman came to my office seeking help. She told me it would be helpful to her to be a part of a group.

Then I reached out to other clients and people I knew to see what they thought of the idea. It got a big thumbs up. I started that group with a few hiccups, but it didn't take long to catch fire.

I evolved it multiple times as new women joined, and my content grew in depth. I created my course Leaders in Love, and added the Women Leaders Alchemy Circle. This lasted for over twelve years!

My "Concept First" experience:

I was so excited about my book *The Soul Search* that I wanted to teach the process and principles to a group. I had the concept all thought out and had already begun creating some parts of the curriculum. I put out an offer to my list and didn't get much response. My marketing message was weak, and I hadn't really identified the problem I would help people solve.

I did finally enroll people in that program and the curriculum was good. However, the participants weren't as engaged and so it wasn't as successful as I had hoped. It came and went.

Later, I did my research and found what my niche really wanted! There WAS a problem they had. They did not have a clear vision for their business. They wanted a vision that was guided by their soul. In addition, they had trouble staying on track with their business and their dream.

OKAY! Now I could work on this concept and create the curriculum knowing what people wanted.

I created a program using the Soul Search process for visioning and called it Destiny Vision Program. It was an instant hit. Curtis and I filled all the available spots in our in-person workshop as well as the private program. It has evolved to be one of our most popular public offerings, Your Business Vision Webinar and Retreat.

If you are choosing a curriculum-based program, you will need to organize and choose exactly what you want to teach or facilitate. This is where you get to bring out (or begin to create) all your resources, exercises, ideas, and inner wisdom.

I have made it super simple for you to do just that with the What Type of Group Suits You exercise below.

BUT FIRST: For any kind of group program, do your research and find out who you think will benefit the most by being engaged in a group program. Identify the type of person you want to work with, and the learning points you most want to deliver in your program. What problem are you helping them solve?

With that as your foundation, you can now organize your information into content and structure. This is where you really get to play around...beginning with the first draft of your program.

I encourage you to put all your ideas into an outline and then play with it. Your play will include deleting, adding, and editing as you continue to discover the best content for your program.

Creating content and structure is where you identify and organize what you will offer in your program.

Like everything else in business building, this is iterative.

You will create many different versions during your career as a coach as you move through the stages of business growth.

What Type of Group Suits You?

Here are the top two types of group coaching and a guide to help you to choose the one that is right for you—the one that will most easily help you grow your business! Read through the descriptions. Soft focus on your niche, what problem they need help solving and how you like to work.

1. Curriculum-Based

This type is based on a curriculum that teaches the participants a skill set around a specific topic. It's usually time-limited, with six weeks being the most common length. It can be held in-person or virtually or a combination of the two.

Curriculum-based groups work well when you:

- Want to become known as an expert
- Want to address a clear problem or teach something concrete
- Want the participants to achieve a specific outcome

2. Process-Based

This type uses a process to support the participants in a particular area of their lives. Its focus is usually broader than curriculum-based groups. It might focus on relationships, business, money, or spirituality.

This type is structured like a mastermind or counseling group. Its purpose is to provide support, learning, and growth in an important area of life.

It can also be used to focus on a more specific niche or problem when combined with the curriculum-based group.

It can be offered as an add-on after a participant has gone through a curriculum-based program.

Hybrid of Both

A process-based group can be combined with a curriculum-based program to help participants move through the issues that arise as the group moves through the curriculum.

The good news is that you can choose to start with one type, or combine them and experiment to see how that works for you.

Now Tune In

Begin by listening to your soul, intuition, and inner wisdom. This will give you information about what type of group you want to offer and to whom you'd like to offer it...your ideal client. What images, ideas and feelings came to mind as you were reading the descriptions, as you were reading this chapter and this book?

After this, you will engage in an activity that I suggest you do on an ongoing basis. Reach out to your target group and find out what they need! What appeals to them? What offering would result in an easy YES, please? Go to webpage EvolveYourCoachingBusiness. com/exercises and download "What Your Client Wants" worksheet.

Content and Structure

It was early fall, and I had that back-to-school feeling. I had been working on my new business academy for coaches and thought I was on the right track with this niche. I just couldn't figure out how to organize all the material and trainings I had created over the years.

I was driving down a beautiful road that leads from the Ojai Valley to the Pacific Ocean. Just as I was cresting the hill and the water came into view, I heard a woman on a podcast talk about content creation and how it worked. My ears perked up.

By the time the ocean was in full view, I felt I had found the holy grail! This woman could help me get past the stuck place that had been driving me crazy.

I pulled into the parking lot where I was picking up a friend, and without any further thought, signed up for this woman's downloadable program.

I was so excited. I was going to get my program together at last! Or so I thought. After plunking down a bunch of money and receiving the program, I found I was more confused than ever. There was a huge workbook and lots of audio recordings to wade through.

Wade through them I did. For three months. No kidding.

It took me that long to realize that what this woman was teaching me was much simpler than she was making it. I learned some things, of course. (One that stuck with me is to name your program something that describes the biggest benefit people will get.)

But I really wasn't any further along on the content creation part except knowing that creating content doesn't need to be that difficult. In fact, it can be simple and people need it to be simple.

When it comes to creating content, the biggest challenge for coaches is usually what to choose, from all the wonderful options you have learned in your training and practice as a coach and beyond.

It is also important to remember you have been trained to hold the space for transformation, to use tools that connect people with their highest potential, to listen, to be curious and present.

All of this is perfect for leading your own groups and creating wonderful programs for your ideal clients. All you need is a little help choosing what to include.

To make it easier for you to do this, I have created an exercise that will help you break down the most important elements of your program.

Exercise: Creating Your Group Coaching Program

Now it's time to begin creating the experience you want for your group coaching offer. Follow this step-by-step guide to build the structure and the curriculum for any type of group you choose to offer.

Write your answers to the following questions.

1. Start mapping out the basic structure of your group coaching program.

    If a curriculum-based program appeals to you:

    *   How long will it last? (e.g., one-time event, six-week course)
    *   How many classes? How often? How long for each?
    *   How will you organize the materials into modules or lessons?

It's okay if you don't know for sure yet, just make up something to get started.

If a process-driven program is calling you:

*   Will it be ongoing or time-limited?
*   How do you want to divide the time?
*   What topics, if any, do you want to include?

For any type of group, you will want to consider how long you want each group meeting to be and how often you will meet.

2. Think about the structure of each meeting, such as having a check in, accountability, or individual sharing. Will there be a time for a topic?

   - How much structure fits with your leadership style?
   - What works best for the people in your niche?
   - What else do you need to consider?

3. Now look at the specific learning points you want your tribe to master or experience as they move through your program.

   Write these down on note cards or pieces of paper. Lay these out in front of you and play around with sequencing them. What's the best order to realize the purpose of your program?

   Remember, you already have much of this information from the previous exercises and your own resources. Take time to review as well as find the new!

4. Using logic and creativity, explore the sequences that make the most sense for your lessons or modules. What structural elements and order will ensure your participants get what you've promised?

   This step may take a while and you don't need to get it right the first time! It usually takes a couple of iterations as you move things around until you feel they're following a natural sequence.

5. What exercises, rituals, books, and other elements do you want to include? What module or lesson will hold them in a curriculum-based structure? How will you add these to your process-based structure? Play with this!

6. Now that you are beginning to see your program take shape, what else might fit? What doesn't fit? What would work better in your next course or in a private session?

7. Do you want to have homework, assignments, or worksheets? If so, look at each module, lesson, or group meeting and think about what would be best to land the learning. Add those into your program!

Put it all together! Construct a first pass at your course content or program structure and see how it flows. Get a sense of the experience it will deliver. Put the program into some kind of form. It may be a bit messy right now, but that doesn't matter. Print your outline and put it into a binder or organize it in a file on your desktop.

Do a happy dance! You have created the content or structure for your coaching program! There will be more versions and refinement of this, but this is a HUGE accomplishment. Celebrate it!

Put it out there!

Each of the steps in the group coaching program exercise will give you a start to creating your content and structure. If you follow all of them, you will have enough to put a date on the calendar to launch your group program! It's time to start making space for it so you can make it real. Once you have this part done, it's time to do some field research to see how it resonates in the marketplace.

Here are some ideas: Reach out to colleagues and clients. Post a simple survey on social media to get a bigger reach. Beta test it by offering a free 90-minute online workshop. This is a great way to test the waters to see what is most impactful in your program. It will also give you clues as to what you most like offering in a group program.

Once you have done your research, you will want to tweak your program to address what your potential participants are looking for.

Exercise: Group Coaching Type

Now that you've nailed down the basics, it's time to deepen your understanding about yourself as a leader and the type of group coaching that suits you and your niche.

Read each question below. Then, stop and observe the answers that come to mind first. Don't think too hard or try to figure it out. You want to tune into your initial, intuitive response.

Write down your answers (even those that may seem outlandish or unrealistic) and then move on. After you have written the answers to each question separately, look at them all together.

Is there something that emerges from these answers that when seen together gives you more clues as to your group offering? Don't worry if it doesn't all fit just yet! This is an iterative process that will evolve over time.

What is your leading style?

Do you love to teach? Would you like to excel in coaching a group? Do you like to provide a lot of materials and information, or would you rather offer a process that allows your group to find their own answers?

Where do you most come alive as a leader?

Is it when you are teaching in front of a room or group? Interacting in a lively way? Telling stories? Or do you get jazzed when listening to others and helping them find new insights?

Which type is right for your niche?

What does your niche need most? Group interaction or tools? What are they already seeking to help them solve their problem? What are they willing to pay for? Will they benefit most from a curriculum-based group? Or is their biggest issue best addressed with a process-based group?

What's the best way to align your group coaching offer with your other services?

What else do you offer or want to offer in your business? Look at the bigger picture of how you intend to increase your income in your business.

Is it through private coaching, retreats, intellectual property? What type of group offering most aligns with your vision for the future growth of your business? Go to webpage EvolveYourCoachingBusiness.com/exercises and download "Get Started Now" chart.

Dynamic Group Leadership

I was sitting in the audience at a learning Center in the middle of Los Angeles. The place was packed with people just like me.

It was late for me to be out in a crowd. I had bucked my usual tendency to turn in early because I was hungry to hear the presenter talk about how I could make passive income in my business.

He held up a CD that contained one of this program offerings and said that most people who bought these (at lectures just like the one I was attending) never even opened them! His point was we didn't need to stress about doing something brilliant, but it was more important how we presented our products.

He created an experience rather than just talking at us. I got how important that was. Using props, such as the CD, brought some entertainment into his talk. Then he did something that really bothered me.

He continued to make this experiential by engaging with the group. He asked us questions and several people raised their hands. One woman took a stab at his question and apparently got the answer wrong. He dismissed her in a way that seemed to me would make her feel ashamed.

I felt the energy sink in the room. He was making this about him. His talk lost its luster. It seemed to me I was not alone in checking out at that moment.

He had made her wrong and he didn't even seem to notice or care about the impact. That ruined the whole evening for me.

I walked out without buying his CD.

That night I learned that when making a presentation or hosting a group learning of any kind creating an experience is important. AND it is essential to be a good leader, to know how to engage your audience or group in a way that makes them feel empowered and not ashamed.

Being a dynamic leader is much like being a masterful coach. You create the conditions for people to learn new things about themselves. It is not about YOU but what you bring out in THEM.

How will you lead a group using your curriculum or process in a way that feels natural to you?

You'll find different ways to interact, engage, and bring your authentic power to a coaching group.

You'll learn the easiest way to keep the group focused and how to engage with participants who are inclined to dominate the group.

You will experiment with:

- What type of group you want to lead
- How to create a dynamic experience for a content-based group
- How to balance heartfelt sharing and forward motion in a process-based group

You will have looked deeper into your own style of leading and what you want to design with your participants, so they know what to expect and are a positive support to each other.

A great place to start is with these questions:

- What do you already know about your effectiveness as a leader?
- What do you admire in other group leaders?
- What have been your favorite experiences in group programs?
- What have been your least favorite experiences?
- When were there times you felt the leader was not doing a great job?

When you look at these and other examples of group coaching, you will find that the qualities that make a group dynamic are often simple.

That is one of the key skills of group leadership—keep it simple and easy to engage.

What makes group coaching leadership fun and challenging is that it is something you can't pin down. There is not a cookie-cutter approach that works for all groups.

Sometimes the challenge is with a group of individuals who have unique ways of engagement.

For some, it's really vulnerable to engage with a group.

This is what makes a group program worthwhile. The participants get to name and move through their resistance, to cultivate vulnerability and learning from each other.

There are some insights and experiential learning moments that can only happen in the context of a group consciousness.

Dynamic Leadership Checklist

The number one way to be a dynamic group leader is to make your program experiential! Below is a checklist of ways to bring your group program to life.

1. Have a Structure

Use time blocks as structures. A time for teaching and a time for interaction. A time for accountability and a time to talk about the homework.

Having a clear structure creates a consistently safe container. The participants can relax into the structure, which allows them to be authentic, access their creativity, and cultivate vulnerability.

2. Have a Clear Beginning and Ending

This makes it much easier for the participants to relax and be present in the moment rather than wondering what's coming next.

It respects people's time. It's professional and creates a container that holds the group solidly.

3. Weave Teaching into the Program

Do this in a way that allows for interaction from the group. It is easy for participants to drift off if too much one-way information is being given without some participation at regular intervals.

This sparks original thinking, invites new insights and curiosity, and brings participants together around a common theme.

4. Have Members Share Respectfully

Guide participants to share within a time limit. Teach them how to give feedback in a way that is empowering. You don't want one person to hijack the group or take up too much time with a story. Clarify the guidelines for sharing and giving feedback as part of your design from the start.

5. Include Simple Interactive Exercises

There is something magical that happens when the group does an exercise together. It doesn't have to be complicated. A simple question to ponder or a coaching wheel exercise followed by each person reporting on their experience.

This engages everyone and sparks an experience of what you are teaching. It can be playful. It gets people's attention and brings an aliveness into the space.

6. Do a Demo or Coach One Person

Sometimes it is useful for participants to go deeper with an issue or to learn something. Coaching and demos bring a program alive and are an effective way to teach or process.

This is like theater. People get to see it happening in the moment, to witness something being created right in front of them.

7. Ask Open-Ended Questions

As coaches, this comes naturally during a private session. It's equally important in a group. Open-ended questions encourage and challenge participants to look for their own answers.

8. Make Right, Reaffirm, Redirect

Sometimes participants will be off base when they share or in their understanding of what you are teaching. The simple response sequence of Make Right, Reaffirm, Redirect will allow you to stay true to what you are teaching and respect the individual who has gotten off track, all the while keeping the class on track.

Example: A participant is telling a story that doesn't relate to the topic at hand.

Let's say the topic is healing and their story takes a left turn.

- **Make Right:** I see how that would be a way to look at it.
- **Reaffirm:** Today the focus is on healing.
- **Redirect:** I'm curious how your story applies to healing?

Having a mix of these elements in your group creates safety and, at the same time, invites full engagement outside the participants' comfort zones. It keeps them (and you!) awake in a way that allows for creativity, learning, and growing.

As you practice these skills, you will discover your strengths and challenges.

Mastering them, you will consistently create powerful transformation through your group coaching. Go to web-page EvolveYourCoachingBusiness.com/exercises "Dynamic Leadership Group Coaching" chart.

Workshop in a Box

One of the easiest ways to give people the experience of group coaching and put a tester out there is to offer a simple online workshop.

Although you can charge for this workshop, I would encourage you to either make it complimentary or hold it as a fundraiser for an organization you care about.

Whichever way you choose, if you do not charge for it, you will still want to put a monetary value on it.

You might say, "*I am offering a workshop, normally valued at $197, at no cost* or *for a love donation to my favorite organization.*"

There are three important elements to this workshop that will ensure it is effective in the way you would like it to be.

1. Choose a focus that ties in with your business and is easy for your niche to understand.

2. Market your workshop! Do the work of getting the word out and promoting the workshop. Advertise it with a compelling topic and great benefits.

3. Deliver a great experience with the promised results.

The marketing you do for your workshop in some ways is more important than the workshop itself!

I have promoted many of this type of workshop and had leads, consultations, and new business come from the promotion itself. Many of these people were not interested in the workshop, but the message I delivered resonated with them.

Of course, you want to deliver a great experience and results.

You also want to leave them wanting more. Weave into the workshop references to clients who have had positive change using the very exercises and concepts you are using.

Keep the workshop simple.

You can get my Workshop in a Box e-book here: EvolveYourCoachingBusiness.com/exercises.

Exercise: Group Coaching Marketing Guide

Below is a framework you can use to create an offer for group coaching or an online program. Write down the headers below and then fill in the blanks. When you are finished, you will have the core of your marketing message and a guide to help you market and enroll your group.

My niche is…

A moment in my ideal participant's life when they need my group program is…

What motivates my ideal participant to pay for the solution I offer is…

The specific problem that is solved by participating in my group program is…

Three core qualities of my ideal participant are…

Three benefits my group program offers are…

Three features my group program offers are…

The people easiest to reach in the marketplace are…

The clearest and shortest path to reach the ideal people and fill my group or program is…

Exercise: Your Program Dream-to-Reality

Remember Mad Libs? Those fill-in-the-blank books that had us captivated on road trips as kids?

Our brains love prompts because they give our brains structure so they can get creative and direct within that structure. Using the answers from the work you've done so far, complete the following sentences. This will Give you a way of holding your vision for success. To make your dream a reality. It will also keep you moving forward from a positive place as you take the steps to promote your group. If one of the sentences doesn't fit, feel free to change it or delete it.

My group program highlights my love of…

And I can't wait to _____ because it brings me alive as a leader.

The people I want to help are _____ because I understand their biggest problems, which are _____, _____, and _____.

The biggest benefits they will receive by participating in my group program are …

The group program will also be enhanced by other services I offer:

1.

2.

3.

I have reached out to people who are ideal for my group, and they tell me the most important things that would help them in their situation are:

1.
2.
3.

I also know from my own experience that it's important for them to learn …

And the transformation that's possible for them is …

Right now, many of these people are weighed down with the problems of _____ and _____.

Their biggest fear is …

And it makes them feel …

In order to help them feel _____ , I will help them solve their problems and achieve their dreams by using the following resources:

1.
2.
3.

I'll call them forward into their greatness by showing them a future-self vision of what's possible for them, which is …

The promise I make to everyone who joins my coaching group or program is …

Take time to feel the truth of this statement. Notice where the juice is when you write and read it to yourself or someone else. Follow that juice!

Nuggets

- The bottom line is this: in order to connect with the marketplace and enroll people in your group coaching program, it is best to have a clear niche so you can speak to them directly.

- For the marketing piece, you can use all the information in this book around your niche, marketing, and stage of business.

- There are many kinds of group programs. Choose one and go with it.

- Get clear on your marketing strategy first.

- Your coaching skills are ideal for delivering a group experience. Use them.

- And…you need to own the leadership role and attitude. You are the leader.

- Don't overthink it. Start out small, go with it, and grow it. *"Done...is better than perfect."*

There are so many ways to grow your business using a group or program! If this is attractive to you, I encourage you to take the time needed to really think this through. Consider the options and then choose one and just do it! Putting a group offering out there will be just what you need to discover what you most want to do in this area and what others most want from you.

Part 7:

KEEP YOUR BUSINESS ALIVE!

We need to accept that we won't always make the right decisions, that we'll screw up royally sometimes - understanding that failure is not the opposite of success - it's part of success.
—Arianna Huffington

The biggest lesson I learned after achieving early success in my business was that it was a living entity that required me to continually evolve it as well as myself. A business is like a child. It needs nourishing and attention in order to keep growing. The good news is that you will learn and grow in wonderful ways as you travel this road.

In this section we will discuss nourishing your business and growing in your power. You will discover what that involves, and ways to improve your learning and growing skills. You will learn new concepts through inspiring stories such as your genius wheelhouse, cleaning your closet, positive pivots, and so much more.

Evolve Your Business

Some of the hardest times in my coaching business came when it was time to make a change. These changes usually came about due to my circumstances changing.

The first challenge came about a year into my first coaching business launch. As you know, I had begun my first business with a niche of entrepreneurs. I hadn't narrowed this niche down beyond people I knew and the people they knew and people who were willing to do the work to achieve their goals.

The inner and outer work! This is still my niche, funny enough, though I have narrowed it down A LOT.

But it was a good enough niche to get my business started. I was known for helping entrepreneurs with time management and helping them navigate the terrain of business building, both the outer challenges and the need for inner confidence and self-love.

So, I made connections with people I knew, went to networking meetings, and did some wacky things like My Front Porch Plan that you read about in the beginning of this book.

I built up my business slowly but surely, to the point of having a solid ten clients and enough successful marketing to keep a few people inquiring on a regular basis.

With this in place, I quit my job working on an executive team for the Postal Service. The golden handcuffs were hard to take off. All those benefits! That great salary! Job security!

But I took the leap, and I will never forget my first official day in my new business. It was about three weeks after the farewell party my former colleagues threw for me.

I had enjoyed relaxing and getting used to NOT going to my job every day. It was a Monday morning and I sat down at my desk. I took out my pretty, dark green business cards, and felt the peace of my choice. I wondered what I would do next. The phone rang.

Miraculously, there was a woman on the other end who was interested in my coaching services! She was a massage therapist and was in my yoga class the previous week and heard me do a little pitch, thanks to my generous yoga teacher.

I told her a bit about my services and then set up a sample session. YAY! I was officially in business. After that moment, I had the inspiration to move forward, and I had faith that my business would continue to flourish.

It did, for a while, until my life took a big turn.

This is when my first husband and I split up, and I moved from my small town to the big town of Los Angeles!

I went through emotional turmoil, physical dislocation, and I needed to take time off to get settled again.

Another day I remember well came about two weeks after I moved to the west coast. I was beginning to feel grounded in my new life. I had a long way to go but I felt ready to reopen my business doors.

I reached out to my clients and thanked them for their patience with the unexpected pause in our coaching.

One by one, I wrote a personal note and sent them an email with an invitation to resume the coaching work.

One by one, I received lovely responses from most of them. The responses had different stories but a common theme.

During the pause they had moved on. Realized they didn't need any more coaching. Found another coach. Not ready to resume just yet...

A few were more personal. They felt let down by me or upset that I would upend my life and was now unreliable. OUCH!

By the time I got to the end of that batch of email responses, I had just a handful of clients left. A small handful, at that.

I no longer had the comfort of a small-town community where I knew everyone and it was easy to make connections. My networking group, my yoga class, and other simple marketing activities were now on the other side of the country.

This was a painful experience to say the least. On top of the grieving I was already experiencing, I now added this loss and had a few good cries.

After picking myself up and dusting myself off, I remembered the saying:

It's the same thing only different.

There were surely yoga studios and networking groups in LA. I knew a few people in town I could connect with.

I also realized I would probably need some of the financial stability I had enjoyed during the launch of my business.

With those lessons in place, I slowly but surely began to do the same things, only different, in my new city.

It did take time and I had many moments where I railed against having to do the same things only different, again and again. Impatience reared its annoying head and there were times I just wanted to give up. It wasn't fair! I had been doing so well. I thought I had it all figured out!

The lessons I took from this experience serve me to this day.

I realized I needed to keep my business alive!

In order to keep it alive, I had to keep doing things that would nourish and grow it, just as I had as a mom to my two amazing children.

If you want to evolve your business, marketing is always necessary, and it doesn't have to be complicated. I learned that running a coaching business requires regular activities to keep new clients flowing in and current clients held by coaching agreements and structures.

The biggest challenge and perhaps the most lasting lesson was this:

There are proven business strategies that work. I have my own way of doing things that I must stay true to. There is a sweet spot where those strategies intersect with fun ways to market. Finding your own way of integrating these and making them your own is the key.

Using these strategies without including your own way never works because it discounts your intuition and creative know-how that will bring new people and opportunities to you every day.

Relying on your way without the structure of proven business strategies means your success will most likely be random and you will have big upsets like the one I encountered during my transition to a new life in Los Angeles.

I can't stress enough the importance of iterating and evolving your business. It is a live entity that requires you to pay attention, pivot, and use your intuition as your guide.

A Positive Pivot

Sometimes a pivot is required because of circumstances beyond your control. Many people had to pivot during the pandemic of

2020. Other times a pivot is necessary because something is not working or there is new information that lets you know it is time for a change.

A pivot in business is not when you make a small change; it is when you move in a new direction altogether.

I want to expand upon a nugget of a story I shared earlier in this book of how I navigated a specific pivot—making a shift that was seismic to my business.

My husband, Curtis, and I were about halfway through our year with a bright vision guiding us forward.

We were on a crusade with our business, which at the time was focused on relationships, spirituality, and personal leadership. This was when we had on our vision board a beautiful rustic church. It was coupled with the words, "We grow our spiritual community."

My ordination as an interfaith minister was hot off the presses at that time and I was expanding my work into areas of new thought ministry, performing weddings, promoting my book the *Soulsearch*, and coaching people on personal leadership.

Then it happened.

The unexpected pivot. Out of the blue, or so it seemed.

I did an exercise developed to guide choices. I was making the choice on what direction to take my business. With all the options I had been experimenting with it felt like time to go in one clear direction.

I put all the options into the matrix of this exercise. All the ones I have mentioned and one more that came to me randomly in the moment. (Pay close attention to those seemingly random options!)

I looked at everything I wanted to do: create community, expand my coaching reach, use my decade of experience as a relationship coach, business coach and Co-Active Training Institute leader, and use my spiritual wisdom. What popped up was a soul-driven business academy for heart-centered coaches. To bring prosperity to the profession I loved the most.

When that choice turned out to be the unexpected winner, you could have knocked me over with a feather. But when I looked closely at what my intuition was guiding me toward, I could see that it made sense.

I wanted to bring what I had learned about succeeding in this profession to other coaches. To bring it with heart and soul as well as business practices that have stood the test of time.

Over the years, I have learned a ton about what works and doesn't work! I have had buckets of fun and plenty of challenges.

Now, with this latest pivot, it seemed as if this was exactly what I had been preparing for all along. Funny how intuition works, isn't it?

It was one big ol' happy day in my world when I connected the dots and saw how I could bring all my passions together.

I did some research and found there was a sweet spot in the marketplace for what I had to offer!

Soul Driven Success – A Business Academy for Life Coaches was born.

With this ONE niche clearly defined, I now support professional coaches with a variety of trainings which help them:

- Grow their business in alignment with their soul's delight
- Facilitate their own coaching groups
- Create content for their programs or inspirational entertainment
- Deliver a ready-made program or add to their own current offerings
- Training for business, spiritual, and relationship coaching!

I tell you this story to show how **ONE niche** can be extraordinarily rich and easily scaled.

One of the paradoxes of having a narrow niche is that it is easier to expand!

Some things to keep in mind:

- Take a look at what you have
- Nothing is ever wasted…repurpose, repurpose, repurpose… you have more than you think you have, guaranteed.
- Iterating a business can be Awesome
- Businesses have stages of growth
- You can't skip a stage!
- It is possible to follow the basic business rules
- AND stay in tune with your own guidance system
- It is worthwhile to keep moving forward toward the sweet spot!

Because I have done my work here and tuned into the inner wisdom as well as the outer feedback, I have landed on a lovely iteration of my business.

You can too!

Wherever you are in your business, there is an iteration you can land on now that will feel good.

I have also just begun to find out what this niche wants. I used the information from my research to launch the first two beta programs and then my yearlong program, my community membership and group coaching masterclass.

You too can move confidently into the marketplace with just enough information to get a foothold. Actually, the only way you will know what works for your niche is to put something out there.

Remember…problems are just the visible tip of a deep, unrealized dream. Helping people reach for their dreams is wicked fun!

To keep your business alive, you need to pay attention to what is happening in your profession and with your niche. It is also important to tune into your own wisdom and listen for those nudges that come.

One inspiring story comes to mind when I look at how important it is to listen to your own wisdom and take the time to grow slowly. That is surely what happened with the craze of the Fuji apple.

The Craze

My first husband, Eddie, was deeply committed to his work. There was a craft to growing fruit that he loved. There was also a commercial side that needed attention if our family was going to eat!

In the early 80s, Eddie received information about the Fuji apple that really excited him. It was immensely popular in Asia, and he felt it would be successful here as well. At the time, Red Delicious, Macintosh, and other apples that had been around a long time were what the growers in our area were planting in their new orchards.

It takes an apple tree about 5-7 years after being planted to really begin producing fruit. Much like many businesses! Much like a coaching business.

He was so passionate about this endeavor that he was able to convince his partners to invest a ton of time and money into planting an orchard of Fuji apple trees. Many of the local growers thought he was crazy. Why mess with a good thing. The popular apples of the day did well enough, and they thought what he was doing was risky.

He trusted his gut and his research. It is that combination that is responsible for most success. He was ahead of the curve on this one, and that too is something to look at in your business. What do you see that is not popular yet, but you have a hunch it will be?

It is like a surfer catching a wave. You have to see it coming and be prepared so you can ride it out. If you are not prepared, it will simply roll right over you.

I have to admit I was not an early adopter when it came to my Eddie's enthusiasm and willingness to risk our financial future on what seemed like a gamble.

I remember people saying things like, *Fuji, what kind of name is that for an apple? That doesn't sound very American.* There will always be doubters in your world. People who won't understand what you are doing or may even try to discourage you from taking an alternative path.

When you listen to your own wisdom AND do your homework AND put in the time and effort it takes to be prepared, you will be like the surfer who catches the wave and gets to ride it all the way to shore. That, my friend, is thrilling!

Eddie was right about the Fuji apple for those reasons. The orchard he planted came into fruition right about the time the Fuji apple craze hit the US big time. He was one of the few growers in our area who caught that wave, so the success was extra sweet.

There is another aspect to this story, and this one is about me and a wave I missed. Because sometimes you won't catch that wave and then you need to know how to recover and pivot your attention to the next wave you see coming.

A few years before writing this book, I got one of those hunches that I described in the introduction of this book. I just knew there was a need for business development for coaches that included soul work.

I felt this was especially true for the Co-Active coaching community I was a part of. Coaches are trained to listen to their inner wisdom, create their life from their values and positive perspectives. To enjoy the experience of life, not just the destination points. I saw that many of the coaches I trained hadn't made these principles a part of their business-building foundation.

I sensed the need and felt my own passion for having a business that aligned with my soul's wisdom. I realized I could narrow my niche and help the people I most wanted to serve. I began building my business academy for coaches. It took about two years to put all the pieces in place. I saw the wave coming and I was preparing for it as fast as I could.

Then COVID-19 hit, and everyone went virtual. My academy was 100% virtual so I was prepared for something I couldn't have seen coming in a million years.

My business did well and started to grow during this time. Much like the Fuji apple story, I had caught the wave and was riding it out.

About halfway to shore on that wave, I got cut off by another surfer. There was another business focused on the exact same niche as I was, that was better prepared and had a stronger foundation, more followers, and other aspects that I had not yet built into my business.

I was having success but there was now BIG competition that I couldn't seem to find my way around.

Here is what I learned from that experience. Sometimes you need to pivot. Let the wave go and regroup.

The business competition that knocked me off my board mid-wave was still gaining new clients and mine were dwindling. I had to find a new strategy.

I took some time to look at what I had and what I wanted to do next. Though it was not an easy time, I found it extremely useful to take stock of my business.

The pivot I made was to let go of things that had seemed like sacred cows. I either no longer loved them or they were no longer attractive in the marketplace. I took into consideration the competition I now had. Not as a negative, but from a positive perspective. If that was what they were doing, how could I align with them, do something different, my own special way or my own unique creation.

Here is the really good news about what happens when you prepare and are intentional in your foundation. Put the building blocks in place that will sustain your coaching business. One more time with the surfing metaphor! You will sometimes be able to catch the wave AND...

There is always a new wave to catch!

Probably more often than you would like, you will miss the wave and someone else will be competing in your own spot on the ocean.

With a strong foundation in place and the habit of listening to your gut and doing your research, you will be able to pivot.

Nothing you have done needs to go to waste. You can use what you have in a new way, bring on partners, let go of things you don't like anymore.

You will be able to keep growing, and most likely grow not just in terms of financial success but also in your joy. Isn't that why you choose this profession in the first place?

The following chapters, each in their own way, will help you stay engaged with your business as a living, growing entity. Your genius wheelhouse, your business designed to suit you, and bringing your own personal values to work. You will learn how to clean out of your closet to make room for all that's next for you.

Your Genius Wheelhouse

A genius wheelhouse is something I call the collection of those essential qualities we all possess that, when identified and utilized, allow us to always be at our best. They bring forth our strengths, gifts, ways of being that just naturally allow us to shine. I like to put these qualities into clear structure so you can picture yourself living into those most positive ways of being.

This idea of focusing on the most positive aspects, and nurturing only those, first showed up on my radar over twenty years ago when I read Julia Cameron's book *The Vein of Gold*. I not only read it, but I also did all the exercises she laid out. My life has never been the same.

I discovered that my own way of navigating in the world worked! I found this to be true the more I owned my unique gifts...whether others thought them to be quirky or brilliant.

I found I did not have to twist myself into a pretzel, compromise my values, or dim my light in order to succeed personally and professionally.

I found my *Genius Wheelhouse*.

Definition of Genius

Exceptional intellectual or creative power, or other natural ability.

Definition of Wheelhouse

Being and doing within one's area of power and excellence.

On a river steamboat (back in the day), a wheelhouse was the casing for the enormous paddle that powered the boat. Anything that fell into that wheelhouse was likely to be struck with incredible force.

In the late 50s this concept was applied to baseball. A ball that was pitched into a hitter's wheelhouse meant it was in the section of the strike zone where the hitter found it easiest to hit the ball.

So, a ball pitched into a hitter's wheelhouse generally resulted in a solid hit and often a home run.

Back to my story…

My newfound wheelhouse wisdom was put to the test right away.

At the time I was still working for the postal service as a mail carrier. This had been a perfect job in so many ways when my kids were small, but now they were older, and I knew I was ready for something else.

I knew what my talents were, and I was determined to find a match in the marketplace.

There is a miracle in knowing and honoring your greatest gifts. This comes in part from the way *knowing* raises your energy! When you operate from your Genius Wheelhouse, you are beaming your greatness and the Universe can't help but respond.

For me, this happened within six months of my learning about my Genius Wheelhouse through the Julia Cameron work I did.

I was hired for a new position working for the Postal Service. My energy was so high, and I was beaming it out. A perfect job was newly created, a job that fit me to a T.

This was repeated a few years later when in my coach training I hit a bump in my Genius Wheelhouse awareness. I did an exercise to identify my true values and had a painful wake-up call as to how often I sold out on them.

The truth is…there are ways of operating in this world that may seem easy because you fit in, it looks good, or it satisfies someone else's idea of what's right. You might even gain great success from twisting yourself into a pretzel or dumbing yourself down a little.

I know, I did.

But eventually you find that it no longer works if your desire is to be fulfilled in your life and your work.

At the Heart of your Business is YOU. It is essential you know your strengths, passions, expertise, and all the good stuff you want to bring to your business endeavor.

I created the Genius Wheelhouse Exercise to make it easy and fun to discover those strengths, both the inner and outer ones. With a visual reminder of who you are at your core and how you best engage with the world, you have a tool to stay on track. The authentic self-expression meets success track!

When you create your Genius Wheelhouse, you will experience a powerful grounding in your strengths that you can use effectively.

It is one thing to know your strengths and another to put them into play in your business.

For this to work, you will need to dig up old assessment results and have fun with some new ones. You will see which ones are most compelling to you today and how they pertain to your business success.

You will reach out to a few people to find out what others think about your superpower and its impact. This is a great way to let people know about your business offering as well.

You will bring forward your past experience and expertise to bolster your confidence and to use in your marketing message.

I use this as a structure with everyone I work with. After showing them all the juicy modules I have in my training program to wet their whistle and assure them we will work on strategy to help them evolve their business, this is the very first thing I do with them.

Before my client and I get down to business, I first want to know who they are and what is in their hearts. Often we tap into wisdom and experience that is brand new to them. The hidden treasures of who they most want to be and are meant to be, expressed through their coaching business.

Now is the time for you to get to know your Genius Wheelhouse as a structure to keep your business alive and to make sure it keeps you continually creating your coaching business.

One sign that indicates you are using the strengths from your Genius Wheelhouse is you may feel vulnerable because you are being true to yourself, especially in your work.

One of my discoveries during a year-long leadership program was that a strength in my Genius Wheelhouse is using humor.

This was hysterical to me because for years I had been working on being more serious and wondering why I wasn't taken seriously! I had been trying to fit into an idea of "how I should be" and it just wasn't working for me... because it wasn't me!

Over the years, I have come to understand that the "how I should be," especially in business, comes from the messages of the dominant masculine paradigm that organizes so much of our work lives.

It can be uncomfortable to be authentic. However, knowing that authenticity is the way to be seen and heard and to have a positive impact on others moved me past my fears.

In order to be vulnerable and authentic, you need to have positive and loving support from others.

The next iteration of my Genius Wheelhouse happened when I did an exercise that required me to ask three people I trusted to tell me what they counted on me for.

I still remember how vulnerable it was to ask and prepare myself to hear the truth. What was especially wonderful about the answers was how consistent they were. Consistent and simple.

At the end of the exercise, we were asked to make a declaration in front of the room using a phrase that began with: *"I promise that in my presence life will show up as...,"* followed by a phrase that we had honed from the feedback.

My promise was:
"I promise that in my presence life will show up as laughter and illumination."

When I made my declaration my whole body tingled! I knew I had found a key component of my Genius Wheelhouse.

I know that people in my tribe who are drawn to the coaching profession are happiest when contributing through meaningful work in the world using their Genius Wheelhouse strengths.

They are not happy just knowing what that genius is. They are not happy making any old kind of contribution. They are not happy contributing to the world without being valued.

They want to earn money for their contribution! The way they contribute needs to be meaningful to them. It is in doing meaningful work that their best is compensated accordingly. That is where a coach's true happiness lies.

Exercise: Your Genius Wheelhouse

The following exercise will guide you to create a one-sheet that anchors you in your Genius Wheelhouse strengths. I think you'll be surprised at the impact this will have on your business and life. It is a simple structure to capture all the most important aspects of who you are at your core, so you can continually evolve your business with authenticity and confidence.

On a blank piece of paper, draw a big circle and divide it into eight segments with lines through the center, like the spokes of a wheel or a big pizza pie with eight slices.

You may recognize this design...it's a simple coaching wheel. Label it *My Genius Wheelhouse.*

You can use this structure throughout your many evolutions of your business, so I encourage you to take some time to make it yours.

Put it in a binder or on a big Post It sheet on the wall. You can also take a picture and use it as a screensaver on your computer. You will use it to check in with your inner guidance system as well as to shape your marketing message.

On the outside rim of each segment, put a label for what's in that segment. You can be creative here. (I have an example at the end of this chapter.)

Inside each segment, put words that represent your strengths, qualities, values, and abilities.

- List your top three experiences which give you credibility in your work. Positions, degrees, certifications, accomplishments, etc.
- Look over assessments you have taken.
- Include concepts, like your Higher Self or Life Purpose that have meaning for you.
- Do the exercises in the following chapters on cleaning out your business closet and personal values.
- Include business values from the previous exercise in the Heart and Soul section.
- Include insights from the Story of Your Life Exercise in the Marketing Your Way section.

Consider your answers to these questions:

- What's working for me as a business owner?
- What inner resources do I have available?
- What outer resources and allies can I count on to support me?
- What are my tangible assets as I move into this business?
- What are my positive thoughts and emotions when I focus on this new endeavor?

This next activity may have the greatest impact on your experience of this exercise, so be sure to include it in your Genius Wheelhouse.

Send an email to (or set up a chat with) five people. Make it a variety of people, those you know personally as well as those with whom you have a professional relationship. Choose people who love you and hold you with a positive regard!

Ask them questions like the following:

- What do you know you can count on me for?
- What is one of my best personal qualities?
- What is my "superpower" in the world?

Feel free to add other questions that tickle your fancy and get to the truth of the impact you have on others.

From all the qualities you have gathered, insert them into the eight categories of your wheel.

You will be referring to it (and definitely tweaking it) throughout your coaching career.

Go to webpage EvolveYourCoachingBusiness.com/exercises and download "Your Genius Wheelhouse".

Cleaning Out Your Business Closet

It was a cold March morning in California. The little nip in the air didn't seem to match the palm trees blowing in the wind outside my window. I had my coffee cup in one hand and a notebook in the other. I was on a mission this morning. I snuggled into my comfy leather sofa and began cleaning out my closet.

The kind of cleaning I was doing, as you might have guessed, was not a REAL closet with coats and boots. This closet was my business closet. Using the metaphor helped me to see in my mind's eye what was happening in my business.

What I was most interested in learning from cleaning this closet was what had been working to keep my business rolling along for many years. It's like cleaning out my actual clothes closet when I want to see what items I actually wear and what looks good on me.

As I snuggled in on that bright spring morning, I started taking things out one by one. What marketing did I like, what services did I most enjoy, where was that sweet spot in the marketplace where I could easily connect with people. That connection allowed me to promote my business in a way that was authentic and kept my integrity in tune with my highest values using my strengths.

For me, it's like that amazing sweater that every time I wear it people tell me it looks great and I always feel good about myself just putting it on. In my business, I had things that often got positive feedback from people such as my blog and my fun quizzes.

One thing I love about any kind of closet cleaning is that, like an archaeological dig, there are always buried treasures. And I find a lot of junk I can let go of, too.

I wanted that kind of clarity in my business, which is why I took a whole day off for this search.

I looked at the people I was working with that I felt were ideal clients. The ones where there was that wonderful chemistry. How had they found out about me?

I looked at the variety of marketing I did to see where the best results were.

I also looked at some of the things I had been learning in a business development course. Things I didn't like to do at all. What about those? Was I being resistant to something that would bring me ideal clients, or was I being wise?

I felt some dread as I began this part of the search. As much as I want to see the truth, I also didn't want to have to do something I didn't like. I was also excited, because at any moment I might find a buried treasure. That sweet spot marketing activity that brought all my strengths together and brought success my way.

As my coffee cup was nearly empty and the sun was rising higher in the sky over the palm trees in my front yard, I saw something. One activity that when I did it my business grew. My business evolved. That one activity was to be in front of a room as a leader. It didn't seem to matter what kind of room, a small networking group, my church congregation, a radio show audience.

This discovery brought both joy and fear. I loved being in front of a room as a leader AND that position was also one that felt really vulnerable to me. I felt my limitations, lack of experience. My inner critic loved telling me I was a fraud when I stepped up to the mic to lead.

There was no question about it, though. This one activity really worked for me. As much as I loved writing my blog and books, creating my deck of cards, and other more introverted things, I couldn't deny what I found in my business closet that day.

The cleaning of the closet story I just relayed happened when I was in the transition from startup to sustainable success stage of my business. I had been engrossed in a business development program that was full of really great ideas and strategies on how to grow my business. Now that I had cleaned out the closet of my business, I could let go of most of them because I saw they hadn't worked for me.

My resistance had been laced with wisdom!

With my buried treasure information in hand, I moved from my comfy sofa to my office desk and started brainstorming about how I could get in front of a room as a leader more often. If that was the number one marketing activity, then it was one I wanted to grow.

That brainstorming led me to another of my favorite activities— Manifesting. I couldn't come up with anything concrete, but I felt a delight at finding a way to be in front of a room as a leader.

I put my full attention on this one thing. I asked for guidance from Spirit. Not a usual business-building kind of thing, you might be thinking. For me, this was also what always worked. Whenever I cleaned out my business closet, I saw Spirit at work in my life.

About two weeks later with spring fully in bloom, I drove along the highway I love most. The Pacific Ocean was on my left with sun shining on the waves, making my heart skip a beat. My heart was also a little skippy because I was going to a big business event in Santa Barbara, which was a thirty-minute drive away, but it felt like a hundred in my heart.

I was going to this event because I had felt that guidance nudging me forward the way it does when my soul wants me to grow. When there is something right for me to do even if I can't see the point.

This was a BIG event with a lot of presenters who knew so much more than I did. There would be hundreds of people there and I didn't know anyone who was attending. Why was I wasting my precious time and money? Putting myself in such an awkward situation for an introvert like me.

I parked in the fancy hotel parking lot. I must have been late because it was hard to find a place to park.

I walked through the lot and, at the entrance to the hotel, I saw the sign for the business convention. The big-name presenters' pictures were on the poster. I wanted to run away. Stupid idea. My cozy coffee-clutching, cleaning-out-the-closet experience seemed far, far away.

I took a deep breath and opened the doors to the convention hall. There were hundreds of women entrepreneurs milling about, chatting, and laughing. Though I felt shy, I also started to relax. These women looked like they were having fun. Right up my alley.

Then I heard particularly warm laughter coming from the table to my right. As I turned my head in that direction, I thought I heard someone call my name.

It couldn't be! I didn't know a single soul here. Maybe the person was calling another Kat.

Then there was a hand wave, my name called again, and a friendly face came into view, smiling from the table where all the laughter was coming from.

There sat my dear friend Sally. We had formed a friendship when she was active in the ICF chapter in Los Angeles. We had enjoyed supporting each other as we began coaching businesses. Sally was a dynamo, and a generous soul as well.

A lot happened at that one event. Sally introduced me to some wonderful women. One of them was a person who had greatly inspired me in her presentation. She also told me about a networking franchise that was brand new. Sally is not one to mince words. She told me I had to do it. To buy a franchise and start my own networking group.

It is exactly right for you she told me, as if she had eavesdropped on my discovery of the buried treasure I found in my business closet.

I felt something kick in when she spoke. I saw I had been guided to the exact perfect place and time to find this offer at the front of the room as a leader position that would be perfect to help me evolve my business into sustainable success. And it did!

A Metaphor that Works

Cleaning out your closet is a metaphor I use to identify what I consider to be one of the BIG spiritual principles that govern our lives…right up there with the Laws of Attraction and the Power of Forgiveness.

This is a necessary and delightful step in any creative process—beginning with what you have.

I first noticed this truth when I was undergoing a spiritual growth spurt many years ago. I was learning about new ways of accessing my power and expressing myself authentically in the world.

As this was happening, and my relationship with others and myself was changing, I was compelled to clear out all the crap in my house!

I went on a tear with this…going so far as hiring someone who specialized in coaching people to let go of stuff they no longer needed or wanted. I cleaned out my basement, my drawers, my garage, and my closets.

I was as ruthless as I had ever been when it came to letting go of things previously thought of as valuable. I was sad to say goodbye to some items, and I was delighted to find treasures I had forgotten—valuables that were hiding among the things I would never, ever need.

When I was finished, I felt freer than I had ever felt before. That lightness carried over into other areas of my life. I lost weight during this time. It just made sense and was not a big deal as it had been in the past.

I let go of ways of eating and foods that were clogging up the works. I saw the value of foods I loved but had not included on a daily basis. My spirit kept getting lighter and clearer.

This was also a time in my life when I was forced to look at some of my relationships that weren't working so well. I needed to do some cleaning up work there too.

I had difficult conversations and experienced painful realizations because now I was more committed to being clean and clear than to holding onto what no longer served my highest good.

A few years later, this same principle became apparent to me in the work I did with my coaching clients. I had a program for entrepreneurs that helped them improve their business in a fun and effective way.

I took people through a process of creating a vision and carrying out a plan of action to make the vision real.

During the "carrying out the plan stage" with my first client, she revealed that she had worked for a corporation for many years in a leadership position.

She had skills, experience, and connections from this work that she had not included in any of our conversations about starting her own business. She thought they were not relevant.

The inclusion of these elements made a HUGE difference in how fast she was able to grow her business. I realized that other clients had their own version of hugely valuable assets they did not consider useful in the context of their current business.

From that moment on, cleaning out the closet has become an important step in every client interaction I have.

The next time this principle showed up in my life was when I was taking a class at my church. One of the steps in this prosperity program was to look at everything I had, and I mean EVERYTHING, in my house, in my head, in my finances, and in my heart.

In this program, it was called the Law of Circulation, a spiritual law that states we must continually clean out what no longer serves us to make way for something better.

Even though I had my previous life-changing experience of cleaning things out and lightening all areas of my life, I saw that I had not made this a regular habit.

I didn't hold onto stuff the way I used to, but I hadn't made it an ongoing practice to look at what I had and make good choices about what works for me now and what needs to go?

When I took on this new habit, once again my life was transformed. It was at that point that I institutionalized this habit in all areas of my life. It's an ongoing process just like brushing my teeth.

I need to do it every day. The areas that are most important to attend to daily are my thoughts. Clearing out my fears, resentments, and limited beliefs, each and every day, leaves me feeling full of joy, no matter what my circumstances are.

That's the kicker for me. We have some idea that it is getting stuff that will make us happy when actually it's being in a flow of giving and receiving that is truly fulfilling.

Cleaning out my financial closet has become a weekly ritual and cleaning out my relationship closet is one I keep an eye on and make sure I assess on a monthly basis at the very least.

There is also the physical cleaning out of my body and of my home. Keeping these sanctuaries clean is one of the easiest ways to stay on track with everything important in my life.

All of this cleaning out works together. I have noticed that when I am cleaning out a physical space, I discover another area that needs to be cleared out.

When I have only what I love and need in my physical space, I naturally am compelled to have only what I love and need in my relationship space…and so it goes.

When it comes to your business, remember that a good place to start is to look at what you have.

So often, we jump over this crucial step. We want things to be different or we want them to remain the same, and either way we don't take the time to see *what we have* so we can make good choices about what to do with it.

There is really no such thing as *don't have*. There are things, experiences, and relationships that we have now and those we desire to have in the future. It's ALL what we HAVE.

The thinking of *don't have* puts us in the territory of lack and limitation. There are always going to be things we can say we don't have…hundreds and millions of things.

Focusing on what we don't have only makes us feel powerless and distracts us from our true creative power. Think about this for a minute.

In a coaching business, it is important to start by looking at what you have now and have experienced in the past that you have carried with you. Look at the experiences you think of as good AND bad, he relationships that have worked out and those that didn't.

Another place that needs cleaning out are dreams you had that never came to fruition. Are you holding onto old dead dreams that will block you from creating new dreams that are even better and more fulfilling?

I encourage you to look around your life, right now, at what you might want to clean out.

Your Business by Design

As I write this, I am once again sitting on a comfy sofa, coffee in hand on a bright spring day in March. My business has evolved a dozen years down the road from when I began the networking group that became so instrumental in my business growth.

Not because that is the best way for you or anyone to grow your business.

Because it was right for me, by design.

This is what I have discovered about evolving a coaching business—you can design it. Like the designed alliance we make with our clients. That design includes what works for you, the coach, and what your client needs. Together you design what works for both of you. It is a wonderous aspect of a coaching relationship. It distinguishes coaches from other professions that are more hierarchically structured.

I recall a moment when my business had been in sustainable success for many years. I realized I wanted something quite different for that stage.

I worked for three years rearranging my business to be the legacy that my heart longed for. The business my soul aligned with, the one that brought me joy because I knew I was helping the right people.

I was working with a business coach who had a program I thought highly of. This program, like the one I had been enrolled in a dozen or so years ago, had a lot of value. But I had hit one of those moments once again when I knew it was time to clean out my business closet. To find the By Design marketing activity that was right for me now.

I had been using all the good advice and wisdom that was being offered to me and some things were working. I had some success, but I wasn't feeling that soul-driven kind of success I wanted my legacy business to have.

By now, I totally trust my gut on this one. All the wisdom in the world is useless to me if it doesn't line up with my own wisdom.

I put everything in my business closet out on the table. I wrote down on little cards everything I had been doing. The marketing, the program I had developed, the branding, the people I served. Then I dug deeper and went searching for buried treasure once again.

I have to admit I was a bit surprised that this cleaning was still such a necessary and powerful exercise. I guess I thought I would outgrow it. I would reach a point where I would know everything. Not so much!

When I cleaned out my closet this time, I saw that the mistake I had been making was thinking that all the online marketing and service delivery changes that had occurred in the past decade had changed what worked for me. I had learned a lot about social media and things like lead magnets (freebies!) and list building.

But when I cleaned out my closet, I saw the same fundamental truth prevailed. For me it was still...get in front of a room as a leader, Kat.

What WAS new this time was how clear the guidance was telling me to do this *my* way.

Use the proven strategy I learned. YES. But take that strategy and get in front of people the way that was most natural for me, not the most conventional way as I was being taught. To come from my most authentic self, using strengths that are inherent and make everything easy. Just as important was what NOT to do. What to stop even thinking about as things I should be doing.

I moved forward with this, and my coach was game to support me in my alternative plan. To create my own small public events, special trainings, intimate online retreats. To go full out on my vision of my business as a boutique business school for coaches. Like one of those hotels I love to go to where there is personal attention, unique furnishings, and spaciousness in the air. Where I can relax.

Once I let go of the conventional way of using the proven strategies, I found the flow that had been missing. My soul was nudging me forward once again to evolve my business along with growing myself into my greatness as a human.

I hope that you too will take the time and make the effort to clean out your business closet. Not just once but regularly so you can experience that tandem growth of business and soul, the creative self-expression that makes having and growing a coaching business so worthwhile—so you too can evolve your business By Design.

Exercise: What Is in Your Business Closet

This is an easy-peasy version to get you started using this business-closet-cleaning tool. It only takes fifteen minutes, and you will learn something worthwhile.

Write down all that comes to mind when you look to the past and present experiences in your business. Take time with each question and listen to your inner wisdom. Allow yourself to be surprised.

1. What experiences are most joyful?
2. What experiences are painful?
3. What are your greatest learnings?
4. What are your fears and doubts?
5. What are you most excited about now?

6. What are you curious about?
7. Where do you feel most alive?
8. What is it time to let go of?
9. What do you want to keep?
10. What is the next best step to take?

Now that you have cleaned out your business closet, what do you have now? Take that next step and keep your business evolving!

Your Personal Values @Work

I agree with Socrates when he said, *"The unexamined life is not worth living."* As well as the words Shakespeare put into Polonius's mouth, *"This above all: to thine own self be true, and it must follow, as the night the day, thou canst not then be false to any man."*

Self-awareness is a life-long journey and there are many ways we come to know ourselves. What makes self-knowledge such an important aspect in having healthy and happy life is this—the better we know ourselves, the more we can trust ourselves to make good choices that are based on our true heart's desire.

Knowing your personal values is an essential aspect of self-knowledge. Connecting these values to your work in the world will ensure you are following your highest path as you grow and evolve your coaching business.

You have your business values which are the values you honor IN running your business. Those values are based on the relationship you have with your business.

Your personal values at WORK help you to stay true to that essential you, the person running that business. They are not about your business at all in some ways, but it can be really helpful to have a deeper understanding of them so you can stay nourished and anchored in your heart as you go about your work each day. This is one more way you can keep your business alive while enjoying the journey.

Much of the struggles and pain in life come from stepping on our values or selling out on what's really important to us.

Personal Values

When you know your personal values, you can honor and live by them.

When you don't, you live by guesswork. Not being conscious and intentional around your values means you are operating blindly.

How do we describe what a personal value is and how it works?

This is a really good question because values, on the one hand, can be elusive and difficult to pin down. On the other hand, when you clearly identify and understand your values, they seem like the most obvious things in the world.

Having said that, here is an introduction to some of the qualities that are shared by all values. There is a list below of many words that have been used to describe values, so you may want to peek at that now to see some examples of what we are talking about.

That list is only a guide. The words you will come up with to describe your values will be unique to you…poetry from your heart.

A value is an essential powerful force in your life, an important idea, concept, or principle that has always, and will always, guide your life. Generally, our most important values are invisible to us, yet ever-present. There is an endless supply of values to be discovered and, when it comes to you and your work, I know there are values just waiting for you to excavate.

Values seem to be consistent throughout a lifetime, although our ways of thinking about, experiencing, and describing them continually change.

One of the ways to discover your values is to notice when you are most alive, excited, and feeling peaceful, grounded, and trustworthy. This feeling comes about when you are living into your values.

When you are cranky, agitated, angry, or bothered by something, it's usually an indication of a value being stepped on.

Here is a story that illustrates how important knowing and honoring your personal values at work can be.

I was in training to teach a coaching certification course. I had been a student in this exact same certification course eight years prior and I had been working full time as a coach ever since. Much of the training was very familiar.

One day, however, we were covering a teaching skill that was brand new to me. I had studied the technique a little, but I knew I would need to practice in order to be good at it. I was feeling tense, so I did some inner exploring.

I knew that, in the past, I had a fear of being humiliated in a learning setting. I have worked hard to always look good and to have the right answers before I open my mouth.

I also knew that wasn't going to work for me this time. A feeling was alerting me to the fact that I was in danger of stepping on two of my highest values, authenticity and playing. As soon as I saw this, the icky feeling disappeared. I knew that if I lived into my values, I would be happy with myself in the class, no matter how I looked to others.

Sure enough, a moment came when they needed a volunteer to do this technique. I raised my hand and played with it full out. I know I fumbled around, did not look good...AND I know I learned, and helped others to learn, this skill because I was honoring my values.

I was completely present to the experience and open to my highest vibration.

Ironically, a short time later I was actually teaching this class and I was being supervised. I had to do that very technique AND my supervisor gave me the highest score possible for being authentic!

The payoff for knowing and honoring your values is multi-faceted and has an impact on those around you. So, remember that when you find yourself cranky, agitated, angry, or triggered it could mean you (or someone else) is stepping on one of your personal values.

Conversely, when you honor your values, you just might find that you are happy beyond reason. Things that you think are going to be hard suddenly become easy.

It is often the simplest things that bring about joy. Knowing and honoring your true values can make this process accessible at any time.

For example, I have a client who has an extremely high value for beauty. For her, it is as simple as giving herself a few minutes in her day to enjoy the natural beauty around her. This simple yet nourishing habit fills up her tank in a way that is beyond reason and very personal to her.

When she takes time to do this before each workday, she has found a profound difference in how her day flows. She calls this value A Beautiful Morning, and sometimes she even sings that song from the musical *Oklahoma!*

It can be fun and helpful when you make up your own names for your values.

Names that make them unique to you. Poetic or fun or dramatic names are good ones to use.

When we honor our values, we increase our own feelings of self-love and the confidence that brings. It can be exactly the lift you need during your workday. It can be like some inner entity is saying, "Good job!"

Exercise: Personal Values @ Work

Look over the list of values below. Think about your daily routine at work and then choose the top three or four that resonate most with you, or feel free to make up some of your own.

When you have chosen your top three, take those words and play around with phrases and similar words that are more meaningful to you or more fun to say and think.

Notice the difference between the times when these values don't show up and when they do. Savor (and keep increasing) the moments they do!

You may already know your values, and as a coach, you also realize that new values are forever showing up depending on the circumstance. Using the following list to get you started, note the personal values you most want to honor in your coaching business.

Personal Values Starter List

Acceptance	Flexibility	Politics
Accomplishment	Forgiveness	Predictability
Acquisition	Freedom	Pride
Adventure	Friendship	Prosperity
Aesthetics	Frugality	Purpose
Affiliation	Fun	Quietness
Authenticity	Generosity	Recognition

Authority	Global Responsibility	Pleasure
Autonomy	Grace	Relationship
Balance	Gratification	Religious
Beauty	Happiness	Respect
Challenge	Harmony	Reciprocity
Commitment	Health	Responsibility
Communication	Helping	Risk-taking
Community	Home	Security
Companionship	Honesty	Self-Awareness
Compassion	Humility	Self-Care
Competence	Humor	Self-discipline
Competition	Idealism	Self-esteem
Conformity	Influence	Self-sufficiency
Connection	Independence	Service to others
Conservation	Insight	Sexuality
Contentment	Integrity	Social Status
Contribution	Intimacy	Socialization
Control Power	Joy	Space
Cooperation	Justice	Spirituality
Creativity	Kindness	Spontaneity
Cultural Heritage	Leadership	Stability
Curiosity	Learning	Structure
Dependability	Listening	Supportability
Diversity	Love	Survival
Differences	Loyalty	Teaching
Duty Education	Meaning	Teamwork
Elegance	Moderation	Time
Emotional Awareness	Morality	Tolerance
Emotional Expression	Mutuality	Tradition
Equity	Nature	Trust
Ethics	Nurturing	Truth

Excitement	Nutrition	Variety
Exploring	Parenting	Wealth
Fairness	Passion	Wholeness
Faith	Peace	Wisdom
Family	Perfection	Wonder
Fitness	Personal Growth	Work
Financial Security	Play	

Add your top Values to your Genius Wheelhouse.

Nuggets

- Make cleaning out your business closet a habit. Continually look at what is working and what isn't and redesign your business to work for you.

- Create and use your own Genius Wheelhouse to keep you focused on your strengths, values, and highest level of wisdom.

- Chances are that in your business, there will be a time when you need to pivot. Stay tuned into yourself and your changing values and to the marketplace and its changing needs.

- When a change knocks you off your feet, shake it off, get up, and make the necessary changes.

- Stay in your Genius Wheelhouse. Come from your strengths and know that when you do that, you will always succeed.

- Do it your way. It's the only way for you to be successful, joyful, and have the impact you want on others.

This section might seem less important than, say, marketing and sales when it comes to your business success. That might be true if what you only cared about was making money. We all know that pursuit alone never adds up to a happy life. When you really honor yourself, your growth, your joy, staying true to your own path, you can have both—a good income and the joy of being on a life journey that includes a business you love. When you combine this with the soul work you need to do in order to stay connected to that wise inner voice, you will have the kind of success you have dreamed of achieving inside and out. More about that in the next section!

Part 8:

SOULWORK

---

*Vulnerability is the birthplace of innovation,
creativity and change.*
—Brene Brown

*The greater the difficulty, the more glory surmounting it.
Skillful pilots gain their reputation from storms
and tempests. Epictetus,*
—Greek Philosopher

In order to evolve your coaching business, you need to evolve and grow yourself at the same time. This requires a commitment to your own personal and spiritual growth to keep moving forward with heart and soul. I have found this to be true for myself and all the coaches I have worked with. When we forget this aspect, our souls let us know! We soon become disillusioned and lose our way.

Take Time to Soul Search

In order to hear that wise inner guide you need to take time to soul search. There are many different ways to do this and I imagine you have a way that works for you.

I came up with my own way, something I call the *Soulsearch* process as a part of my own growth and at a time when it was sink or swim for my coaching business. I have written a book (available on Amazon) on the topic and it is one of my favorite trainings to deliver.

The story below highlights how important soul searching can be when you are working to create a business that is successful. It was sent to me by one of the participants in a challenge I lead, using the Soulsearch process to increase income.

Dear Kat,

I started out wanting to increase my income through my new business. Though I signed up for your 90-day challenge and was willing to give it all I had, I really never thought it would happen. I not only wanted more income, I also really wanted to THRIVE in my business.

I had the passion and was willing to do the hard work but had never been able to make a living that would help support my family. That piece had been missing since I left the corporate world. My husband always believed in me, but it took a long time for me to find a belief in myself.

Using the Soulsearch every day made a serious impact on my business. It took time, but in six months my business started to take off! Over that period of time, I felt a major shift in my thinking. I went from doubt and a vague idea of what I wanted to serious clarity.

The picture of what I wanted was so clear I could feel it. That feeling was so good that it fueled me to release some of the crap that was getting in the way. I had some clearing out of an old business to do in order to fully focus on my new business. I was able to let go of the fear that was tied to the things that reminded me of the failure of that business. The weight of that failure was released, and I was able to let go of my shame.

The end results were astounding. In six months, I had more than doubled my income! Beyond miraculous!!! The wonderful part was that I was no longer struggling. I wasn't forcing anything. Things just started flowing. I had talked for a year about offerings I wanted to create, and all of a sudden people were showing up wanting those exact offerings.

If I were to bottom-line what happened, I'd say I connected to myself on a deeper level. It was a process wherein I started to trust God and life and where I moved into the flow of divine assistance. Another big growth for me was becoming masterful in my work as a coach. There was a spiritual alignment with these clients.

I achieved the success I aimed for. The Soulsearch helped me move past a period of overwhelm that came with all the new responsibilities. I learned that I could trust myself, even when I was in emotional pain. And that I would come out on the other side and be OK. I now know I will always be OK. Always be OK. That changes my whole relationship with life. Now, is that worthwhile? Damn right it is!

—One Happy Coach

I wholeheartedly agree with this coach. Taking time to reflect and connect with your soul is worthwhile for so many reasons. If you need a refresher on ways to soul search, here are some building blocks that I find useful.

1. Time set aside with no obligations
2. Alone or with another in a structured process
3. An inquiry or set of questions about the topic you want insight on
4. No set outcome. No urgency. No judgement.
5. Open to whatever comes even if you don't like it
6. Listen for clues that may come in unusual ways

I find journaling, walking in nature are helpful to dip into a place where I can here beyond the chatter of my mind. An art project also can help unlock your inner wisdom. One of my favorite ways of soul searching is to walk a labyrinth. One easy way to do this is to download a labyrinth image and instructions that are available online and print them up. Then use your finger to trace to pattern following the labyrinth searching your soul.

However you choose to do your soul searching, it is important to make time and create a regular ritual of listening to that wise inner voice. That voice that connects you to the wisdom of your soul. This is where your wisdom comes into play in helping you succeed from your soul.

This is a quite different kind of success than the kind that comes just from your mind. Soul searching gives you access to that inner voice that has your best interests at heart. The part of you that can then channel your wisdom into creative action based on what is most important to you at any given time.

Soul searching should be done on an ongoing basis to keep you on track and connect that wisdom with proven business strategies. This is the winning combination.

Here is the process we use on a daily basis, and the book we wrote about it. Go to webpage EvolveYourCoachingBusiness. com/exercises and download"the Soulsearch Process" worksheet and book.

Tangled Thinking

Sometimes with all the stuff coming at us on any given day it is easy to get what I call Tangled Thinking. This kind of thinking mixes up the true and false, good and bad, into a big knot. When you have this kind of thinking going on, you feel stuck.

There is a simple way to soul search when you are stuck. When you feel you have a challenge that you just can't seem to gain clarity on. When you bounce back and forth in your mind with thoughts that get you all tangled up.

For good reason, I call this exercise Untangle Your Thinking! This exercise is something to grab when tangled thinking hits and you need an in-the-moment soul searching tool. Go to web-page EvolveYourCoachingBusiness.com/exercises and download "Untangle Your Thinking" eBook.

Your Mountain to Climb

The metaphor of a Mountain to Climb came to me when I realized that I kept facing and overcoming challenges as the CEO of my business. I encountered and overcame these challenges because there I was pursuing something that really mattered to me. Much like a mountain climber, seeking fulfillment from taking on something challenging that had a compelling reward at the top.

There have been many mountains I have climbed in the twenty years I have been a coach. One mountain in particular stands out for me because I climbed it more than once.

I love creating deep and meaningful relationships with people. This is one of my greatest strengths. The mountain to climb stems from the relationships I have with my clients. I love the wonderful people I work with and the deep connection we have. This is why I became a coach.

But that same exact quality can get in my way when I put TOO MUCH focus on them and forget what is important to me.

I stood at the foot of this mountain during the winter I was completing my interfaith seminary. My experience in seminary was blissful and expanded me as nothing ever had before. I would say it was one of the most rewarding and perfect learning experiences I ever had.

During my seminary years, I wrote my first book and began delivering talks to my spiritual community. I was finding my voice during this time. The spiritual training helped me to anchor in my soul's wisdom and follow the teachers who had paved the way for my self-expression.

I had maintained my coaching business, which was doing very well. I had a full roster of clients and three ongoing coaching circles. I had a wonderful experience creating and leading a relationship program called Leaders in Love with Curtis and my dear friend Abigail.

You may recall this to be the time I described briefly before. Business was booming…but I was not happy. Something in me had awakened and I just couldn't ignore it. I had evolved and now I was ready to evolve my coaching business. It was time. The mountain before me was…*Stay true to myself while honoring the love I have for the people currently in my community.*

This mountain I had to climb would require that I hold onto the love of the people but let go of the form my business would take. This mountain climbing, like all mountain climbing, real or metaphorical, requires you to go into the unknown. To face challenges that you can't predict or plan for. I knew I had to climb this mountain. My soul was urging me to a greater expression of myself.

I was afraid. I knew I had to keep an eye on this fear.

The fear of losing people. Fear of letting people down. Fear of disappointing people. Fear of being rejected. Does any of that sound familiar to you? Maybe you have your own version of fears that crop up when you are ready to expand.

As I began to climb this mountain, I saw that the change in my business structure was going to be dramatic this time. It was beyond the incremental changes I had made in the past. Beyond a price increase or a new way of doing things. This mountain landscape was devoid of all clients. In order to make the big change my soul was seeking, I had to let go of all my private client work for now.

I didn't have much time to contemplate this because as my seminary was coming to an end, and I knew I wanted to devote myself to my studies in a way I hadn't been able to before. This was my opportunity to fully immerse myself in the spiritual training that was feeding me.

I took a BIG gulp. I spent a week considering and crafting a message to all of my clients. Then I gave the message some love, and hit send. I was now on a rocky part of the mountain, and I knew it. What would people say, how would they respond? How would I deal with the loss myself?

At times, I was holding on for dear life on the cliff's edge. Yes, I know this may sound dramatic, but that is how fear operates. The drama was also coming from my growth into new territory. I knew I needed to keep an eye on this fear in order to keep moving forward.

Keep An Eye on Fear

When you keep an eye on fear and keep putting one foot in front of the other, this kind of mountain climbing will expand and grow you in the best possible ways. What really helped me continue walking and expanding on this climb was when I tuned into my intuition, my inner guidance, and felt just how right this choice was for me. I also found I could stay true to myself and give a little on my timeframe.

Fear makes us rigid. It turns the color spectrum into just black and white, and narrows our vision.

Keeping an eye on my fear, I just let myself notice how much I might want to shut down, just give in, or plow mindlessly ahead.

It wasn't easy to get to the top of that mountain. It took much longer than I had imagined to close my private client practice. I lost some wonderful clients who disappeared forever and that hurt.

But then the dust settled, and I planted my flag on top of that mountain.

When I stood in front of a church in the middle of New York City that June as an ordained interfaith minister.

When a year later as I reopened my business doors, I realized I was happy I had done the climbing.

I could feel the expansion that had happened in me and was excited about what was next. I had stayed true to myself and the people I loved. Now some of them were coming back and there were many new people to love.

And it turned out that what was next was the best evolution of my coaching business EVER. One that makes me super happy to this day.

A coaching business is a noble pursuit. Different from other types of business, it requires an investment of more than just time and money. To really enjoy your success in this profession you need to put your heart and soul in it.

That is how mountain climbing works in this business. Your fears may look completely different than mine. Or they may be similar. The key is to notice the fear and look for the gift in the challenge you face. Look at the mountain in front of you as the path to your growth and your business evolution.

Your work here is to look at what you need to grow in yourself, the challenges you need to meet and master in order to reach the destination you are aiming for in your business.

Your mountain to climb can be soul-based and exciting Your soul simply wants you to expand into greater and greater expressions of yourself. Greater and greater expressions of love and joy. Soul does not care a whit about how things look or your level of comfort!

Your mountain to climb is an intentional adventure. It requires courage and conviction. It requires that you know your purpose and what is so important that you are willing to take a risk. Climbing a mountain is risky business, for sure!

You need to be prepared and you need to receive support from other people and from Spirit. It requires believing in yourself enough to make it through the rough patches. This is all possible when you keep remembering your purpose—the reason you want to achieve that dream.

For coaches, the reason is usually threefold. You want to succeed in your business, you want to feel the joy doing this work, AND you want to have a positive impact on your clients and the world! For those reasons, your mountain to climb can feel exciting rather than scary. Your success is waiting for you at the top of that mountain—and so are a bunch of people who need your help!

Exercise: The Keep an Eye on Fear

Anything done from the heart will include fear and the whispering (or perhaps shouting) from your saboteur. To help you manage this, I have created a cool exercise you can use anytime that fear arises. You can't eliminate fear, but I have found that when you keep an eye on it, you can manage and move past even the scariest places on your journey to success.

Have handy three pieces of paper and a pen.

Take a moment to imagine you have accomplished your coaching business vision. Imagine yourself planting a flag on top of a mountain in celebration of this achievement!

Notice how it feels. Enjoy the view.

Let the feeling of accomplishment fully sink in.

Now take a piece of paper and label it "Ego-Based Fear." Begin to list all the fears, worries, and limited beliefs that get triggered when you think of accomplishing your goals and creating your vision.

1. As you write the words on this piece of paper, make it very clear to yourself that these thoughts are simply thoughts. Label them as "Ego-Based Fearful Thoughts that get in the way of me accomplishing my purpose."

2. Let your mind know, in whatever way works for you, that these are fears, distortions, distractions, rabbit holes of negative energy, that sneaky saboteur trying to stop you.

3. Remind yourself that their sole purpose is to keep you safe and comfortable. Bless them for that!! And notice

how they do it in a way that actually constricts and limits your true self.

4. As you write down each, label them clearly as blocking you from achieving your success. Don't spend a lot of time thinking or engaging in any emotion here. Keep it moving in a matter-of-fact manner.

5. Put it all out there and label it accurately—in your mind and on the paper. You are using a skill called "Name It to Tame It," which triggers an important neurological response in your brain.

6. When you are done labelling, turn over that piece of paper. Make sure you turn it over intentionally and consciously, feeling yourself as separate from those labeled entities. The mind takes visual cues quite literally and will know by this action to let go and move forward.

Now you get to take a look at the challenges in your life that have taught you the greatest lessons.

Using another sheet of paper, write down the top three challenges you have faced in your life.

These are the ones from which you came away a better version of yourself. Overcoming these challenges grew you into a stronger and wiser person.

Now focus on the challenges you are currently facing. Write them down.

Notice what it feels like as you shift your focus back and forth between the past challenges, which grew you into who you are now, and the present challenges, which are here to grow you into the person you are becoming.

These challenges are way stations on "Your Mountain to Climb," put there so you will learn and grow into a better version of yourself right now!!

Take a third piece of paper and label it "My Soul's Expansion." Write on this piece of paper whatever comes into your mind as you explore these questions:

1. What are the mountains I need to climb in order to achieve my goals in my coaching business?

2. What will I learn?

3. What qualities will I need to embody in order to reach the top?

4. What will I discover that inspires me about myself?

5. Who will I be after I climbed my mountain?

Go back to the very beginning of this exercise and allow yourself to steep more thoroughly in the feeling of having climbed this mountain. Notice what you are most proud of and most delighted to have accomplished.

Nuggets

- Bestselling author and life coach Martha Beck said something years ago that has stuck with me: "You have to live it to give it." Do the work on yourself to stay present and healthy in your life and your coaching business.

- Fear is a natural part of this work. Learn to recognize its many faces, accept the impact it will have on you, and learn to shift out of it as soon as you can.

- Make a clear distinction between the kind of fear that will only take you out and your mountain to climb, which is the personal growth work necessary to experience soul driven success. Choose the mountain and keep your eye on fear.

- Know that the impact of your coaching business is serving a high purpose in the world.

- Keep untangling your thinking. Clarity is your greatest ally and will serve you well.

- Develop a habit of searching your soul, daily if possible, so that you keep the channel to your soul open.

This book began with a chapter intended to anchor you in an inspiring vision, fueled by your values and connected to what is important to you as the foundation for building a coaching business. Knowing how to evolve this business requires all I have covered here. Ways of thinking that make it possible for you to pivot when needed, make little and big changes to stay on track with the marketplace as well as your soul's purpose. Coming from your strengths is one key but also so important is being realistic about the personal growth work needed to keep clear of the blocks and to move past the obstacles that are not only probable but inevitable on this type of journey. Along with soul searching, the other essential ingredient in a happy work life is a community of kindred spirits!

Part 9:

THE VALUE OF COMMUNITY

Alone we can do little: together we can do so much.
—Helen Keller

There is no power for change greater than a community discovering what it cares about.
—Margaret J Wheatley

Alone we go fast, Together we go far

It was a cold December morning. An east coast winter day was blooming, which meant I was all bundled up with gloves and a scarf and my warm fuzzy boots. I was not alone in this attire. As I look around the hotel conference room, many others were shedding coats and piling them up on the chairs which formed a circle in the center of the space.

I was nervous to be here at last and so grateful that my best friend Corinne had tagged along, even though she had no interest in becoming a coach.

She told me she knew I would be learning a new language in my coach training, and she wanted to be able to understand this world I was entering.

When I looked across the room, there she was talking to a group of people already! Me, well I am much more shy when first getting to know folks. I held back a little and was glad when the leaders took their places at the front of the room.

I relaxed and took out my notebook and pen, ready to take notes in my introverted way. No such luck.

Before my butt had even warmed the seat we were up and doing a mingle. It was then that it struck me. As I spoke to each person and saw them up close and personal, I thought...these people are all on a similar path as I am.

We are doing this together. They are nervous and excited too.

That was my first coaching training course at the Coaches Training Institute. By the end of that weekend, I not only was hooked on becoming a coach, but I had a very unexpected experience of being a part of a community of kindred spirits.

It was this community that helped me through the rough patches of my training. The personal transformation that occurred was life changing in ways that challenged my very foundation.

This community held me, encouraged me, challenged me every step of the way.

I had been a lone wolf when it concerned my personal and professional growth. Allowing only a few folks into my inner sanctum. Even those, I kept at arm's length when I felt too vulnerable.

I learned in my coach training experience that community makes all the difference. The difference between "learning" in an intellectual way and really learning in a holistic way that brought me out of my shell and into a much fuller experience of life.

I became a bit of a training junkie for a while in order to BE in a community. I joined ICF shortly after I moved from Gettysburg to Los Angeles.

I walked into that first ICF meeting free of the shyness that had previously held me back. I knew there would be supportive people there. Some of the people I met at my very first meeting are still my friends to this day, as a matter of fact. We still support each other.

In Los Angeles, I joined a spiritual community, the Agape Spiritual Center. It was here that I found my spiritual nourishment and once again found a community to belong to. I found my first office on the bulletin board there. I joined Mark Victor Hansen's entrepreneur program, which included a wonderful yearlong community experience.

Office Hours

I dialed the number and waited. Standing in the hallway, a bit in the shadows, leaning against the wall. I had been seeking privacy to make this call because I was nervous. A coach friend of mine had suggested I make this call.

He thought there was a potential kindred spirit attached to the number I was dialing which belonged to a friend of his. Calling someone out of the blue brought my shyness back to the surface.

I was relieved to be sent to voicemail.

This was one of those experiences that taught me how important it is to get out of my comfort zone to make a connection.

The woman whose number I called that day was a kindred spirit in so many ways! When Laura and I met in person, just a few days after she returned my phone call, I realized we shared a lot of common values.

We shared a love of coaching and a desire to connect with other entrepreneurs instead of trying to do it all alone.

We met often to brainstorm about our coaching businesses and found it so beneficial to have each other's support. We decided it would be fun to invite others.

We started something we called "Office Hours." We invited all the coaches we knew to come to my house every Wednesday afternoon. The idea was to have a combination of support and simply doing some of the tasks with a supportive community.

I honestly don't think I could have made it through some of the most challenging times I faced in my startup stage without Laura and some of the wonderful people we gathered in those office-hour meetings.

When I look at my current business, I see people connected to the wonderful kindred spirits in the communities I was part of.

A Dream Come True

When I moved to Ventura to live by the ocean, which was a dream come true, again I sought community.

I found a Unity church which fed my soul and my need to be a part of something bigger than myself. Once again, I found the benefits to be abundant.

In my first month at that church, I was asked to do a workshop based on the five love languages. I got to experience leading that wonderful community myself. The minister of that church was the person who encouraged me to start my own community. My first coaching circle.

I joined a movement class and found another wonderful community with a leader who became my client and then a dear friend.

I went to a few networking meetings and then formed my own networking group.

People Who Care

The community I had engaged with in Los Angeles continues to this day to be a support in my life. I found people there who cared about me and were on a similar path of caring about our world and wanting to make a positive difference. Together we DO go far.

For example, Laura partnered me on one of my radio shows and even traveled with me to Virginia once, where we did a show exploring the impact of a mass shooting. She also is one of the editors of this book!

It was in that Los Angeles community that I met Sally, who later helped me start my own networking group. Someone who came to the very first Office Hour, a man named Brad, became my friend and, for a time, my business partner in a program called Nail Your Niche, Land Your Brand, which was the beginning of my current program for coaches!

And many, many more people from these, and other communities I have joined since, are the cheerleaders who help me evolve my coaching business to this day.

This is something I can't stress enough, as you evolve your business and your own personal growth, you too need community.

You could apply everything written in this book, but without a community to support you, it won't flourish nearly as fully without those kindred spirits cheering you on.

This is how it works. When you are a part of a community of kindred spirits you will be held and supported. You will also reap the benefits that come with the connections you make. The heart connections, as well as the ones that bring you new business.

My love of community has grown to the point where I am always engaged as a member of a community in order to be supported and make those wonderful connections. I am also the leader of my own community, which has become my greatest joy as a coach.

For you, it may be the same or completely different. You may, like me, find that leading a community floats your boat. You may want to stick to being a coach with one-on-one clients or some combination of the two.

Whatever you choose as you move forward, be sure that you have support so you can and will go far.

Engage with your Communities

As a business person, it is important to belong to a variety of communities. These can be both local and virtual. Local communities may include regular Meetup groups, Chambers of Commerce, yoga studios, spiritual organizations, and coach gatherings, such as ICF chapters.

They can also include communities with which you share a passion such as writing, reading, hiking, or a creative art. In these communities, you can foster relationships, receive great referrals, and get different kinds of support for yourself and your business.

There are many online communities with which you can engage: coaching, financial growth, business development, or personal growth. You engage with kindred spirits who want to support you and your business, as you will support them and theirs. It's win-win.

There are also communities such as ours, Soul Driven Success, which are intended to mentor and support you and your business. Here, you can participate in mastermind groups, make connections, and share a similar journey. Go to webpage EvolveYourCoachingBusiness.com/exercises.

Nuggets

- We are a social species. Isolation is unhealthy. The time of the Lone Wolf is over. Find your communities and use them well.

- Community is essential for coaches in business. It will support you, challenge you, and nourish your soul.

- Receiving and giving support with kindred spirits not only feeds the soul, but it's also really good for your business.

- It is easy to isolate yourself. Watch out!

- It is always worthwhile to seek out and experience the huge benefits of community.

- Find the communities that work for you. If you can't find one, create one and start inviting others to join you.

TO YOUR PROSPERITY

Congratulations! You have devoted precious time and energy reading this book and doing exercises that will evolve your coaching business. You are making a difference in this world with your work. Creating prosperity through good work is a noble and fulfilling experience. I encourage you to use all you learned in this book to keep growing yourself and to evolve your coaching business to be prosperous and have the positive impact this world needs more than ever.

I have done my best to bring the stories, examples, and exercises to both inspire you to keep growing in your business and as a human, but also to give you the steps to take and keep taking. Keep this book handy as you move into action, and please reach out to my online community for support or to further your learning of any aspect in this book. I wish you soul-driven success in your business and in your life.

With love,
Kat

ACKNOWLEDGEMENTS

There are so many people who contributed to this book. I know I will miss some! There are those who stood by me personally and cheered me on when the going got tough. My husband, Curtis, leads that pack. His devotion to my writing and our message at Soul Driven Success has been invaluable to this whole journey.

My amazing children Laurel, Devon, Emily, and Nathan for their loving and ongoing encouragement. I am especially grateful to Laurel who, while on a road trip, sang me right through some tricky editing and Devon who gave me advice that took me over the finish line with the cover.

My sister Gretchen who talked me through many of the aspects and listened to me process and always cheered me on. As did my dear friends, Jodi, Cathy, Corinne and Abigail.

My wonderful publisher Jesse who guided me with his good nature and wisdom. The hard working and talented editors, the marketing team and design crew at Lifestyle Entrepreneurs Press.

A very special thanks on bended knee to my friend and editor extraordinaire Laura Lallone. This book would not be what it is if not for her genius touch.

All coaches need coaches, mentors, and guides. I have been fortunate to have many wonderful people in my corner. A few that helped me as I was preparing to write this book and helped me to move forward are Jeff, Mark, and Barbara.

Then there is my own community of coaches who gave me encouragement every step of the way. The larger community of my colleagues and fellow coaches from the Co-Active Training Institute who supported me in so many ways!

Last but not least to all of you wonderful people who took part in my crowdfunding campaign to get this book off the ground. Abigail, Prout, Amanda, Kessler, Amanda, Barry, Angela, Long, Ann, Vanino, Beverly, Doman, Brad, Stauffer, Candace, Seniw, Carmen, Tarbell, Cathy, Norman, Christopher, Esposito, Connie, McIntyre, Devon, Rankin, Dorrie, Aldrich, Emily, Kisner, Gina, Howell, Gretchen, Richmond, Haley, Hoekstra, Jodi, Bogart, Karen Lovelace, Tofte, Kat, Knecht CPCC PCC, Kim, Kassnove, KS, LIM, Laurel, Rankin, Leesl, Herman, Lisa, Kramer, Margo, Huennekens, Marie-Elizabeth, Mali, Mark, Sieverkropp, Maureen, Johnstone, May, Samali, Merreley, Donohue, Natalie, Hill, Nathan, Knecht, Patricia, McGraw, Riem, Elfar, Rohini, Duvvuri, Sandy, Pruessner, Sarah, Nordhausen, Stephanie, Lovinger, Summer, Siino, Susan, Viglione, Tanya, Bugbee, Tisha, Marina, Tracy, Collier, Wilhelmus, Peters, William, Barr